Coastal Rail Termini
of Britain and Ireland

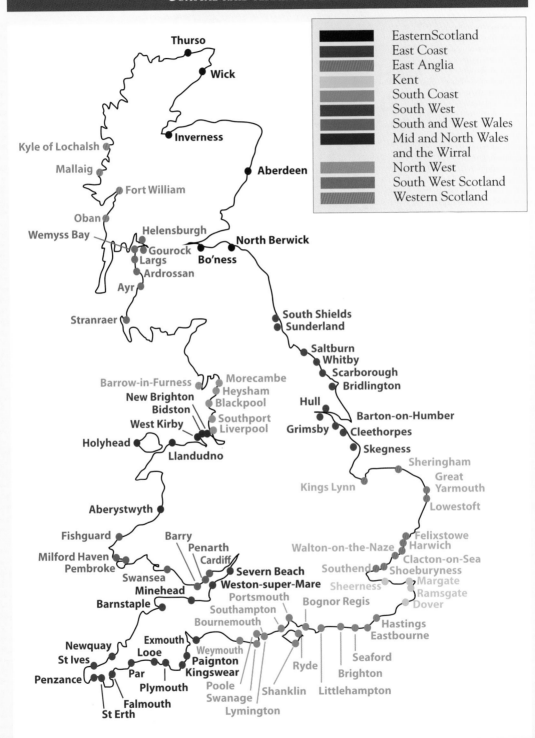

Thurso
Wick
Kyle of Lochalsh
Mallaig
Inverness
Fort William
Oban
Aberdeen
Wemyss Bay
Helensburgh
North Berwick
Gourock
Largs
Bo'ness
Ardrossan
Ayr
Stranraer
South Shields
Sunderland
Saltburn
Whitby
Scarborough
Morecambe
Bridlington
Barrow-in-Furness
Heysham
New Brighton
Blackpool
Hull
Bidston
Southport
Barton-on-Humber
West Kirby
Liverpool
Grimsby
Cleethorpes
Holyhead
Llandudno
Skegness
Sheringham
Great
Yarmouth
Kings Lynn
Lowestoft
Aberystwyth
Felixstowe
Fishguard
Barry
Harwich
Milford Haven
Penarth
Walton-on-the-Naze
Clacton-on-Sea
Pembroke
Cardiff
Southend
Shoeburyness
Swansea
Severn Beach
Sheerness
Margate
Minehead
Weston-super-Mare
Ramsgate
Barnstaple
Portsmouth
Bognor Regis
Dover
Southampton
Hastings
Bournemouth
Eastbourne
Newquay
Exmouth
Weymouth
Seaford
St Ives
Looe
Paignton
Ryde
Par
Kingswear
Brighton
Penzance
Plymouth
Poole
Shanklin
Littlehampton
Falmouth
Swanage
St Erth
Lymington

EasternScotland
East Coast
East Anglia
Kent
South Coast
South West
South and West Wales
Mid and North Wales
and the Wirral
North West
South West Scotland
Western Scotland

SEE ALSO MAP OF IRELAND TERMINI ON PAGE 4

Coastal Rail Termini
of Britain and Ireland

A gazetteer of all current standard gauge coastal
and estuarine termini

John Hillmer

Silver Link Publishing Ltd

First published in 2012

British Library Cataloguing in Publication Data

A catalogue record for this book is available from the British Library.

ISBN 978 1 85794 363 4

Silver Link Publishing Ltd
The Trundle
Ringstead Road
Great Addington
Kettering
Northants NN14 4BW

Tel/Fax: 01536 330588
email: sales@nostalgiacollection.com
Website: www.nostalgiacollection.com

Printed and bound in the Czech Republic

COASTAL RAIL TERMINI OF IRELAND

Portrush
Londonderry   Larne

Belfast   Bangor

Ballina   Sligo

Westport

Drogheda

Galway

Howth
Dublin
Bray
Greystones

Limerick

Tralee   Waterford   Rosslare

Cobh
Cork

Northern Ireland
Republic of Ireland

Half title This wonderful view is looking down on Fishguard station on 18 September 2010, occupied by Pathfinder Tours' 'The Western Wales Explorer' special, topped and tailed by Class 66 No 66015 (this end) and 'Deltic' No 55022 *Royal Scots Grey. Adrian Kenny*

Title page The entrance to Portsmouth Harbour station on 31 August 2011. *Anthony W. Smith*

Contents

Acknowledgements

My sincere thanks go to all those who have been so helpful with photographs and/or information: Hugh Ballantyne, I. S. Carr, Richard Carr of SAYLSA, Mark Chatterton, Roger Cornfoot, Matthew Crockett, Matt Davies, Neil Dinnen, David Evans, John Furneval, Mark Hillmer, Richard Hillmer, Adrian Kenny, Neville Knight, John McCrickard, Roger Marks, Mike Mensing, Brian Mills, Brian Morrison, Finbarr O'Neill, David Panton, John Robinson, Keith Sanders, Paul Shannon, Geoff Sheppard, John Simms (West Somerset Railway), Anthony W. Smith, Howard Sprenger (RAILDATE), Gwyn Taylor-Williams, Mark Thomas of Pembrokeshire County Council (Museums), and Peter Townsend of Silver Link.

Particular thanks to Chris Playfair, for all his help with information and the photos he supplied of Northern Ireland and the Irish Republic, and to Terry Gough, not only for his photographs but for his careful advice. Also to my wife Geraldine for all the support she has given me, particularly in the preparation of images for publication.

Abbreviations

ATW Arriva Trains Wales (TOC)
BR British Railways (including British Railways Board, British Transport Commission, British Rail, etc)
c2c Part of National Express Group (TOC)
CIE Coras Iompair Eireann
DART Dublin Area Rapid Transport
DMU Diesel multiple unit
EM East Midlands Trains (TOC)
EMU Electric multiple unit
FC First Capital Connect (TOC)
GC Grand Central (TOC)
GR East Coast (TOC)
GW First Great Western (TOC)
GWR Great Western Railway
LB&SCR London, Brighton & South Coast Railway
LM London Midland (TOC)
LMSR London Midland & Scottish Railway
LNER London & North Eastern Railway
LNWR London & North Western Railway

LSWR London & South Western Railway
LUAS Dublin light rail
LYR Lancashire & Yorkshire Railway
MR Midland Railway
NER North Eastern Railway
NEXUS Newcastle and area local transport undertaking
NIR Northern Ireland Railways
NR Network Rail
NSE Network South East
NT Northern Rail Ltd (TOC)
P&DSR Paignton & Dartmouth Steam Railway & Riverboat Company
ScR First ScotRail (TOC)
SN Southern (TOC)
SR Southern Railway
SW South West Trains (TOC)
TOC Train Operating Company (post-privatisation)
TP First TransPennine Express (TOC)
VoR Vale of Rheidol Railway
VT Virgin Trains (TOC)
WCML West Coast Main Line
XC CrossCountry (TOC)

Bibliography

Baker, S. K. *Rail Atlas of Great Britain and Ireland*, 11th edition (Oxford Publishing Company)

Bradford-Mitchell *Rail Times* 22.5.11 to 10.12.11 (Middleton Press)

Butt, R. V. J. *The Directory of Railway Stations* (Patrick Stephens Ltd)

Fox & Pritchard *Irish Railways* (Platform 5 Publishing Ltd)

GB Rail Timetable, Winter Edition 12, 11.12.11 to 13.05.12 (The Stationery Office)

Hillmer, John *Gazetteer of the Railways of Wales* (Silver Link Publishing Ltd)

Marsden, Colin J. *Rail Guide 2010* (Ian Allan Publishing Ltd)

Quail Track Diagrams No 1 Scotland & the Isle of Man
No 2 Eastern (TRACKmaps)
No 3 Western (TRACKmaps)
No 4 Midlands & North West
No 5 Southern & TfL

Quick, Michael *Railway Passenger Stations in Great Britain – a Chronology*

Wikipedia (where each station in the UK and Ireland has its own individual page)

Introduction

There is something rather special and exciting about a coastal terminus, and all those included are within 1 mile of the sea or estuary. The size of the station does not matter – it is where trains end their journey, and passengers often continue by sea or by air (Penzance offers this alternative). At some trains arrive at the buffers, then reverse out to continue their journey – Fort William and Inverness are two examples. Others are through stations, but are included because some services regularly terminate there – Aberdeen and Dover Priory are two such. Several stations are more estuarine than by the open sea, but have also been included – Liverpool Lime Street on the Mersey, Bo'ness on the Firth of Forth, and Barton-on-Humber are in this category.

The stations are presented in a geographical sequence starting in the north-east of Scotland at Thurso, then down the east coasts of Scotland and England, along the south coast of England to Penzance, then along the north coasts of Cornwall, Devon and Somerset to the Bristol Channel. We then move along the south coast of South Wales to Pembrokeshire, the Welsh coast to Aberystwyth and Pwllheli to Anglesey, and the North Wales coast line to Llandudno. The Wirral peninsula follows, then north to Southport and up the west coast of England into Scotland and to Kyle of Lochalsh. We finally cross the Irish Sea to take in Northern Ireland and the Irish Republic.

While every effort has been made to include photographs that portray the stations as they are today, changes are happening all the time and I apologise for any where the scene has changed since publication.

John Hillmer
Wilmslow

Notes

- The number beside the station name is the page number in *Rail Atlas: Great Britain & Ireland* by S. K. Baker.

- 'P&P' refers to inclusion in the relevant volume of the 'British Railways Past and Present' series published by Past & Present Publishing Ltd.

- Under 'Services', timetable references and details of train services refer to Bradford-Mitchell's *Rail Times*, 22 May to 10 December 2011 (Middleton Press) and the TSO *GB Rail Timetable*, 11 December 2011 to 13 May 2012. Times and service frequencies change, so the details given must be considered as variable.

- Figures for annual passenger usage can be obtained from the website of ORR (Office of Rail Regulation) at : www.rail-reg.gov.uk/upload/xls/station_usage_0910.xls

'So bracing!' This statue at Skegness station, photographed on 18 September 2010, is based on the famous figure of the 'Jolly Fisherman', commissioned in 1908 by the Great Northern Railway and widely used to advertise the resort on the company's posters. *John Robinson*

Eastern Scotland

Opened	28 July 1874
Original company	Sutherland & Caithness Railway
Subsequent owner	Highland Railway; LMSR; BR
Currently managed by	First ScotRail
Station code	THS
Platforms in use	One
Position	Northern terminus of branch line from Georgemas Junction
Services	Table 239: through services from Inverness/Dingwall, four on Monday-Saturday and one on Sunday.
Notes	Northernmost station in UK. Trains reverse and continue to Wick, so Thurso is technically not a terminus.

Above: On 24 September 1980 Class 26 No 26042 leaves for Georgemas Junction. Until the arrival of the 'Sprinters', all services from Inverness divided into two portions at Georgemas Junction, one each for Thurso and Wick. The train loco worked through to Wick with a separate Class 26 working the Thurso portion from Georgemas Junction. *Paul Shannon*

*Belowe:*Class 158 No 158703 (based at Inverness) is seen on 23 October 2010. Since 1980 the layout has been simplified, with the siding on the left having been removed. *Peter Townsend*

WICK   88

Opened	28 July 1874
Original company	Sutherland & Caithness Railway
Subsequent owners	Highland Railway; LMSR; BR
Currently managed by	First ScotRail
Station code	WCK
Platforms in use	One
Position	Terminus for trains from Inverness, having called at Thurso
Services	Table 239: four trains on Monday-Saturday from Inverness/ Dingwall and one on Sunday.

Above: On 14 August 1976 Class 26 No 26044 stands with a service to Georgemas Junction. *Paul Shannon*

Below: Apart from the small trainshed itself little has remained the same in the 34 years between the two photographs. On 23 October 2010 there are two Class 158s (Nos 158703 and 720), both based at Inverness, side-by-side in the station, although only the left-hand platform is used by passengers. There are also two short sidings further to the right. *Peter Townsend*

Left: The exterior of the station, also 23 October 2010. *Peter Townsend*

INVERNESS   88

Opened	5 November 1855
Original company	Inverness & Nairn Railway
Subsequent owners	Highland Railway; LMSR; BR
Currently managed by	First ScotRail
Station code	INV
Platforms in use	Seven
Position	Terminus for trains from Aberdeen, Kyle of Lochalsh and the Far North Line from Thurso and Wick, and sleepers from Euston.
Services	Table 229: from Edinburgh and Glasgow Queen Street. Table 239: from Wick & Thurso, and from Kyle of Lochalsh. Table 240: from Aberdeen. Table 403: 'Caledonian' sleeper from Euston. Table 26: 'Highland Chieftain' from King's Cross, the only non-First ScotRail service, operated by East Coast.

Above: The sleeper from Euston (leaving there at 2110) has just arrived at Platform 1 on 18 August 1997. The four trainsheds can be seen – Platforms 1-4/5 cater for the services from the south, whilst 4/5-7 deal with northbound trains. *Author*

Above: Also on 18 August 1997 we see three units – (left to right) BREL 'Express' Class 158 No 158706 forming the 1043 to Aberdeen, 'Super Sprinter' Class 156 No 156485 forming the 1105 to Wick, and sister unit No 156493 as the 1045 to Kyle of Lochalsh. *Author*

The scene has not changed on 22 June 2004, as Class 158s Nos 158718 and 158732 await departure as the 1040 to Edinburgh. *Hugh Ballantyne*

ABERDEEN   86

Opened	4 November 1867 as Aberdeen Joint Station Committee (replacing previous stations at Guild Street and Waterloo); rebuilt 1913-16; renamed Aberdeen 1952; major refurbishment 2007-08
Original companies	Caledonian Railway and Great North of Scotland Railway
Subsequent owners	LNER and LMSR; BR
Currently managed by	First ScotRail
Station code	ABD
Platforms in use	Seven/eight (Platforms 6 and 7 are through platforms with South and North sections; 3, 4 and 5 are terminal platforms)
Position	Most services from both north and south terminate, except some from Inverurie and Dyce to Edinburgh and the sleeper from Euston to Inverness
Services	Table 26: to King's Cross (GR). Table 51: to Penzance (XC), the longest journey in the UK. Table 65: sleeper between Inverness and Euston (ScR) and services on WCML. Table 229: to Glasgow Queen St and Edinburgh. (ScR & GR). Table 240 to Inverness, some to Dyce and/or Inverurie (ScR). Table 402: sleeper to Euston (ScR).

Above: Class 47 No 47786 heads the 2140 sleeper service to Euston on 16 July 1999. *Hugh Ballantyne*

Above: Aberdeen's attractive foyer. *Mark Hillmer*

Above: Two Class 170/4 'Turbostars' stand at bay Platforms 3 and 4 on the same day. *Mark Hillmer*

BO'NESS (heritage line) 78

Opened	10 June 1856 (original station approximately quarter of a mile west)
Closed	7 May 1956
Reopened	1981 (new station)
Original company	Slamannan & Borrowstounness Railway
Subsequent owners	North British Railway; LNER; BR
Current owner	Bo'ness & Kinneil Railway (Scottish Railway Preservation Society)
Platforms in use	Two
Position	Terminus and HQ of heritage line
Services	Trains run between Bo'ness and Birkhill with one intermediate station at Kinneil Halt.
Notes	Line is 3½ miles long. Station buildings were brought together in 1980s from various places, guaranteeing their preservation. Trainshed is of most importance, having been transported from Edinburgh Haymarket.

Left: Ex-LNER 'D49' 4-4-0 No 246 *Morayshire*, designed by Nigel Gresley and built in 1927/28, awaits departure to Birkhill on 5 August 2007. *Author*

Below: Virtually the same scene four years later sees Class 37 No 37906 at the Class 37 Gala on 3 January 2011. Built at the English Electric Vulcan Foundry in November 1963, the locomotive is now powered by a Ruston engine. *Keith Sanders*

NORTH BERWICK   79

Opened	17 June 1850; enlarged 1894 to cope with increased traffic
Original company	North British Railway
Subsequent owners	LNER; BR
Currently managed by	First ScotRail
Station code	NBW
Platforms in use	One
Position	Terminus of line from Edinburgh, leaving main line at Drem Junction
P&P	No 9, pp15-16
Services	Table 238: from Haymarket and/or Waverley, with a reduced service on Sundays. A few trains start back from Glasgow Central.
Notes	Station has suffered periods of decline – it was on the 'Beeching' hit-list and in the Serpell Report in 1982, but survived both, and is now thriving, although in 1985 buildings were demolished and remaining platform reduced in length. Line from Drem Junction electrified in late 1990s; regular services commenced 8 July 1991.

Above: Class 380 'Desiro' No 380106 forms a return service to Edinburgh on 14 July 2011. *Keith Sanders*

A most attractive small boat full of flowers is located by the entrance to the station, photographed on 19 July 2010. *Keith Sanders*

East Coast

Opened	24 March 1984
Original company	Tyne & Wear (Nexus)
Currently managed by	Tyne & Wear (Nexus)
Station code	SSS
Platforms in use	One
Position	Terminus of branch line from Pelaw
Services	Map of Nexus on p20 of *Rail Times*
Notes	Station is 100 yards south of original, which opened on 2 June 1879 (NER) and closed 1 June 1981 (BR). New station is situated on bridge above King Street, principal shopping street of South Shields, close by Kepple Street bus station.

Top right: At South Shields old station on 6 January 1963, looking towards the Tyne, an EMU is ready to depart for Newcastle. All has now been demolished. *I. S. Carr, courtesy of The Armstrong Trust*

Middle: Looking towards the end of the line on 8 July 2011. *Terry Gough*

Right: Taken on the same rather wet day, this photograph is looking towards the end of the line, where there are several engineering sidings. *Terry Gough*

SUNDERLAND   76

Opened	3 August 1879, replacing earlier stations at Hendon and Fawcett Street; new station known as Sunderland Central; modernised 1965; refurbishment commenced 2008.
Original company	North Eastern Railway
Subsequent owners	LNER; BR
Currently managed by	Northern Rail/Tyne & Wear (Nexus)
Station code	SUN
Platforms in use	Four (one large island platform)
Position	Although a through station between Heworth and Seaham, on both Network Rail and the Tyne & Wear Metro from Newcastle to South Hylton, it serves as a terminus for King's Cross trains
P&P	No 4, p62
Services	Table 26: to King's Cross (GC). Table 44: Hexham line/Metrocentre/ Newcastle to Middlesbrough. Table 48: to Hexham.
Note	One of few stations in UK where both heavy and light rail services share same platform.

Above: This view was taken on 29 April 1958 and shows the station how it used to be prior to modernisation. Looking towards the far end of the platform there is some similarity with the modern picture below. The loco is ex-LNER 'G5' 0-4-4T No 67253. *I. S. Carr, courtesy of The Armstrong Trust*

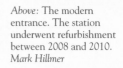

Above: The modern entrance. The station underwent refurbishment between 2008 and 2010. *Mark Hillmer*

Left: Looking along Platforms 1 and 2, towards St Peter's, on the right is the 'light wall' with individual LED units containing an animated display by Jason Bruges Studio. *Mark Hillmer*

SALTBURN   68

Opened	19 August 1861; known as Saltburn-by-Sea/Saltburn-by-the-Sea until 1887/89
Original company	Stockton & Darlington Railway
Subsequent owners	North Eastern Railway; LNER; BR
Currently managed by	Northern Rail
Station code	SLB
Platforms in use	Two
Position	Terminus of branch line from Middlesbrough
Services	Table 44: regular services from Bishop Auckland/Darlington/Middlesbrough.
Note	Once four platforms and various carriage sidings for excursion traffic, etc.

Above: Standing at one of the remaining platforms Class 153 No 153315 forms the 1430 to Bishop Auckland on 2 November 1999. Over the years the station has been reduced in size. *Author*

Above: The reduction can be judged by the substantial original entrance to the station, which survives although now in different use. *Author*

Looking towards the buffer stop on Platform 2 on 20 January 2011, there has been very little change since 1999, other than perhaps the colour of the waiting shelter! *Mark Hillmer*

Above: The most attractive wrought-iron entrance leading to the platforms – No 1 is on the right and No 2 on the left. *Author*

WHITBY   69

Opened	4 June 1847; originally opened as horse-drawn tram system on 8 June 1835 (Whitby & Pickering Railway, engineered by George Stephenson; at one time known as Whitby Town
Original company	York & North Midland Railway
Subsequent owners	North Eastern Railway; LNER; BR
Currently managed by	Northern Rail
Station code	WTB
Platforms in use	One
Position	End of branch line from Middlesbrough. Also used by North Yorkshire Moors Railway (heritage line) for limited number of services from Pickering since April 2007
Services	Table 45: Middlesbrough to Whitby, Monday to Saturday, reduced service on Sunday.
Note	Over the years station has been considerably reduced in size to current single platform.

Above: This photograph from 25 August 1975 shows a much larger station than remains today. Two platforms are in use, with a bay on the right. The units are both Class 101s. *Author*

Above: By 25 September 1993 many changes have taken place. Class 156 No 156444 stands at the remaining platform forming a Middlesbrough-bound service. *Author*

Above: On 23 October 2010 the original station entrance has survived, although put to other use. *Author*

Left: The return of steam-hauled services from the North Yorkshire Moors Railway attracts a great deal of attention. On 23 October 2010 an ex-LMS 'Black 5' is bringing in a service from Grosmont, where the NYMR line joins the Network Rail branch from Middlesbrough. *Author*

SCARBOROUGH   69

Opened	8 July 1845; previously known as Scarborough Central to distinguish it from Scarborough Londesborough Road on York line, which subsequently closed in 1963
Original company	York & North Midland Railway
Subsequent owners	North Eastern Railway; LNER; BR
Currently managed by	First TransPennine Express
Station code	SCA
Platforms in use	Five
Position	Terminus of branches from York and (via Seamer West Junction) from Hull
Services	Table 39: from Liverpool Lime Street or Manchester Airport (First TransPennine Express). Table 43: from Hull and beyond to Sheffield (Northern).

Above: The clock tower and fine exterior of the station are seen on 29 July 2010. *Author*

Below right: Looking west from the buffers on 29 July 2010, Platform No 1 is on the extreme right; it is reputed to have the longest station platform seat in the world! A Class 185 is approaching with a service from Manchester. Falsgrave signal box is in the distance on Platform 1, together with a fine signal gantry; the latter has since been dismantled for subsequent re-erection at Grosmont on the North Yorkshire Moors Railway, but the future of the box is uncertain. *Author*

Left: This view from 20 October 2007 shows the shorter four of the five platforms with the station entrance clock tower in the background. *John Robinson*

BRIDLINGTON   63

Opened	7 October 1846
Original company	York & North Midland Railway
Subsequent owners	North Eastern Railway; LNER; BR
Currently managed by	Northern Rail
Station code	BDT
Platforms in use	Three
Position	Although on through line from Scarborough to Hull, station is also terminus of some services from Hull originating at Sheffield/ Doncaster
P&P	No 25, pp126-137
Services	Table 43: Scarborough-Hull/Doncaster/Sheffield.
Note	Station has most wonderful floral displays externally and in entrance/concourse area.

Above: The station frontage on 29 July 2010. *Author*

Above: The wonderful floral displays in the entrance hall and foyer, seen on 29 July 2010, offer a great welcome to arriving passengers. *Author*

Inside the station on 13 February 1996, Class 142 No 142087 awaits departure to Hull at Platform 6. To the left are the two through platforms for Scarborough services. *Author*

HULL PARAGON INTERCHANGE 63

Opened	8 May 1848 (officially 1851) as Hull Paragon
Original company	York & North Midland Railway
Subsequent owners	North Eastern Railway; LNER; BR
Currently managed by	First TransPennine Express
Station code	HUL
Platforms in use	Seven
Position	Terminus of lines from Leeds/Selby and from Scarborough/Bridlington
P&P	No 25, pp55-59
Services	Table 26: to Kings Cross (First Hull Trains). Table 29: various services from Sheffield/Doncaster or Liverpool/Manchester/Selby (TP). Table 33: all services from York (NT). Table 39: all services from Manchester (TP). Table 43: all services from Scarborough/Bridlington/Beverley (NT).
Note	Official opening of new transport interchange by HM the Queen and Duke of Edinburgh 5 March 2009.

Above: In this overall view of the station on 13 February 1996 Class 158 No 158776 is leaving for Manchester Piccadilly. There appear to be nine platforms available, and little has changed in the intervening years. *Author*

Above: The bus and rail stations have been integrated; in this view from 24 November 2010 the length of the entrance can be seen, with the buses at the far end. *Author*

Class 158 No 158855 is ready for departure with a Northern Trains service. The view is looking along the length of the platforms from the buffers, on 24 November 2010. *Author*

BARTON-ON-HUMBER   63

Opened	1 March 1849
Closed	1 June 1981
Re-opened	24 June 1981
Original company	Great Grimsby & Sheffield Junction/Manchester, Sheffield & Lincolnshire Railway
Subsequent owners	Great Central Railway; LNER; BR
Currently managed by	Northern Rail
Station code	BAU
Platforms in use	One
Position	On Humber Estuary, terminus of branch from Ulceby
Services	Table 29: basically a 2-hourly service from Cleethorpes, Monday-Saturday, with no service on Sunday in the current Winter timetable.
Note	Connecting bus service from town to Hull, which replaced New Holland ferry.

Above: A plaque commemorating the 150th anniversary of the first public train into Barton-upon-Humber on 1 March 1849. *Author*

Above: The mini-interchange for trains and buses, seen on 24 November 2010. *Author*

Looking towards the end of the line on the same day. *Author*

GRIMSBY TOWN   64

Opened	1 March 1848 as (Great) Grimsby; 'Town' added 1900
Original company	Great Central Railway
Subsequent owners	LNER; BR
Currently managed by	First TransPennine Express
Station code	GMB
Platforms in use	Three
Position	Through station between Habrough and Cleethorpes
P&P	No 27, pp8, 40-42
Services	Table 27: trains terminating from Newark North Gate/ Lincoln (EM). Table 29: Manchester Airport to Cleethorpes (TP), Cleethorpes to Barton-on-Humber (NT).
Note	The station was refurbished in 2007/08.

Above: A Class 114 'Derby Heavyweight' DMU (leading vehicle E56014) leaves with an afternoon service from Cleethorpes to New Holland on Saturday 20 March 1976. *Michael Mensing*

Above: The station entrance, seen on 21 January 2010, has benefited from refurbishment with a modernised booking office and café facilities. *Author*

Left: A Class 185 DMU is about to leave with a Cleethorpes to Manchester Airport service on 21 January 2010. Comparison with the 1976 photo shows that the roof has been completely replaced with a modern structure. The line to the right is the terminal bay used by the East Midlands service from Newark North Gate/Lincoln. *Author*

Left: This 21 January 2010 view of the station looking west was taken from near Garden Street signal box, which, although closed, remains in situ. Towards Cleethorpes the line becomes single. *Author*

CLEETHORPES   64

Opened	6 April 1863
Original company	Manchester, Sheffield & Lincolnshire Railway
Subsequent owners	Great Central Railway; LNER; BR
Currently managed by	First TransPennine Express
Station code	CLE
Platforms in use	Three
Position	Terminus of all trains from Grimsby
P&P	No 27, p46
Services	Table 27: from Newark North Gate/Lincoln (EM). Table 29: from Manchester Airport/Sheffield. Table 30: from Barton-on-Humber (NT).

Above: The rather unusual entrance to the station, photographed on 21 July 1998. *Author*

Above: Looking from the buffers on the same day, two of the three platforms are in use. On the extreme left is Class 158 No 158764 with the 1129 service to Manchester Airport, and at Platform 3 is Class 153 No 153378 with the 1100 to Barton-on-Humber. *Author*

A 'Desiro' Class 185 stands at Platform 1 with a First TransPennine service to Manchester Airport, looking towards the buffers at the end of the platform on 21 January 2011. *Author*

Above: The departure screen on 21 January 2011. *Author*

SKEGNESS 55

Opened	28 July 1873
Original company	Wainfleet & Firsby Railway
Subsequent owners	Great Northern Railway; LNER; BR
Currently managed by	East Midlands Trains
Station code	SKG
Platforms in use	Four
Position	Terminus of line from Sleaford/Boston
P&P	No 27, pp110-11
Services	Table 19: nearly all services are from Nottingham, calling at Grantham for East Coast Main Line connections.
Note	A station refurbishment is due for completion early in 2012.

Above: On 3 November 1998 Class 156 No 156419 stands at Platform 4 out of the six then available (there is no Platform 1), forming the 1218 service to Manchester Airport. *Author*

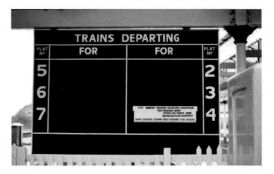

Above: The departure board in November 1998 was pretty basic! *Author*

The day a 'Hastings' came to town! On 18 September 2010 preserved unit No 1001 operated a special to Skegness (1Z44), having left Hastings at 0637. To the left is Class 158 No 158773 at Platform 3. *John Robinson*

Two Class 365 units stand in the station (No 365531 to the left and 510 to the right), awaiting their turns to King's Cross. The view is looking towards the buffers on 29 September 2005. *Brian Morrison*

KINGS LYNN   44

Opened	27 October 1846 as 'Lynn'; resited 1871; renamed to present title 1 January 1911
Original company	Lynn & Dereham Railway
Subsequent owners	Great Eastern Railway; LNER; BR
Currently managed by	First Capital Connect
Station code	KLN
Platforms in use	Two
Position	Terminus of main line from London via Cambridge/Ely
P&P	No 12, pp26-27
Services	Table 17: from King's Cross primarily, or Liverpool Street.

Above: On 29 July 1979 we see the single-line station 'throat' with a Class 47 at the head a London-bound service. On the left-hand side is the stabling point, with Class 37 No 37036 (of March depot) visible, and out of view a Class 03 (primarily for use in the docks) and a Class 08. At that time there were semaphore signals in use at the station. *Author*

Right: The station frontage on 16 October 2011. *Author*

SHERINGHAM (North Norfolk Railway)   56

Opened	16 June 1887 as 'Sherringham'; renamed to current spelling in 1897
Closed	2 January 1967
Reopened	c1970
Original company	Eastern & Midlands Railway, merged in 1893 with Midland & Great Northern Joint Railway
Subsequent owners	LNER; BR
Currently owned by	North Norfolk Railway
Platforms in use	Three
Position	Eastern terminus of the North Norfolk Railway heritage line
Services	To western end of line at Holt.
Note	Station reconnected to remaining line to Norwich (see overleaf) 11 March 2010.

The entrance to the station on 17 October 2011. *Author*

Below: Since the 1970s the line, running to Weybourne and Holt, has prospered. Standing at the main platform on 30 June 2010 is Waggon & Maschinenbau Railbus No 79960, complete with 'speed whiskers'! *Author*

Inset left: Not many years after the reopening of the line, ex-LNER 'B12' 4-6-0 No 61572 is stabled by Sheringham station on 13 May 1979. *Author*

SHERINGHAM   56
(Bittern Line)

Opened	2 January 1967
Original company	BR
Currently managed by	National Express East Anglia
Station code	SHM
Platforms in use	One
Position	Terminus of branch line from Norwich
P&P	No 12, p117
Services	Table 16: services from Norwich, Monday-Saturday, with reduced service on Sundays.
Note	The link between the two stations at Sheringham was opened on 11 March 2010.

Above left: On 13 July 1980 a Class 104 DMU has just arrived from Norwich. *Author*

Above: The view towards the buffers at Sheringham on 29 June 1980. At this time a road divided the two stations – the North Norfolk heritage line can be seen in the distance. *Author*

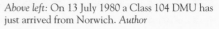

Left: Looking east along the new connection between Sheringham (North Norfolk Railway) and Sheringham (Network Rail) on 17 October 2011, a Class 156 unit is working the branch from Norwich. *Author*

GREAT YARMOUTH 46

Opened	1 May 1844; became Yarmouth Vauxhall before current title adopted
Original company	Yarmouth & Norwich Railway
Subsequent owners	Great Eastern Railway; LNER; BR
Currently managed by	National Express East Anglia
Station code	GYM
Platforms in use	Four
Position	Terminus of direct line from Brundall via Acle and indirect line via Reedham and Berney Arms
Services	Table 15: regular services from Norwich on the direct line and very infrequent services via Berney Arms.
Note	Station was badly damaged during the Second World War and rebuilt in 1960. There are plans to further update it.

Top: While it was still called Yarmouth Vauxhall, on 10 March 1979, a Class 100/105 (Gloucester/ Cravens) DMU forms the 1350 service leaving for Norwich (via Acle), while Class 37 No 37047 is stabled at Platform 1, having brought in an excursion train. *Michael Mensing*

Above: By the time this photo was taken on 8 June 2000 the station had been refurbished, and a Class 170 No 170204 stands in the same position at Platform 3 with a Norwich service. *Author*

Left: Class 156 No 156407 arrives at Platform 2 from Norwich on 18 October 2011. *Author*

Below left: The station entrance on 18 October 2011. *Author*

Below: The modern glass end of the concourse, seen on 18 October 2011. *Author*

Below right: A plaque commemorating 2 June 1940 when, under threat of invasion and air raids, five special trains evacuated children and teachers to the Midlands. Yarmouth was subsequently heavily bombed. *Author*

LOWESTOFT   46

Opened	1 July 1847; known as Central from 1903 to 1971
Original company	Norwich Railway
Subsequent owners	Great Eastern Railway; LNER; BR
Currently managed by	National Express East Anglia
Station code	LWT
Platforms in use	Three, two of which are in regular use
Position	Terminus of lines from Norwich via Oulton Broad North and from Ipswich via Oulton Broad South
Services	Table 13: from Ipswich via Woodbridge (East Suffolk Line). Table 15: from Norwich (Wherry Line).

Above left: Still retaining the 'Lowestoft Central' exterior nameboard early in 1978, this view shows the original entrance to the station. *Author*

Above right: On 13 May 1980 a Class 105 DMU awaits departure time for Ipswich. There were three platforms in use at that time. *Author*

Middle left: By 2007 the trainsheds had been removed. On 4 August 2007 Platform 2 is occupied by Class 170 No 170205, having arrived from Liverpool Street, while at Platform 3 is Class 156 No 156402, forming a service to Norwich. There is no Platform 1. *Brian Morrison*

Left: Looking towards the buffers on 4 August 2007, unit No 170205 is at Platform 2. Compared with the 1980 view, a number of buildings to the rear remain the same, in particular chimney pots on the left and the flat top of the central building in the background. *Brian Morrison*

FELIXSTOWE   38

Opened	1 July 1898 as Felixstowe Town; changed to current title in 1969
Original company	Great Eastern Railway
Subsequent owners	LNER; BR
Currently managed by	National Express East Anglia
Station code	FLX
Platforms in use	One
Position	Terminus of branch from Westerfield
P&P	No 12, p62
Services	Table 13: services from Ipswich.
Note	Station is on other side of car park from original.

Above: This old part of the station is now in a shopping centre called 'Great Eastern Square' and a car park, as seen on 4 April 2011. *Anthony W. Smith*

Above right: Class 153 No 153354 stands at the buffers and will form a return service to Ipswich on 4 April 2011. *Anthony W. Smith*

Right: The view of the part of the station that remains in use, with a Class 153 awaiting departure. *Anthony W. Smith*

HARWICH INTERNATIONAL   37

Opened	15 March 1883 as Parkeston Quay; replaced by new passenger terminal 1972; renamed Harwich International Port 1995, although 'Port' dropped from the title shortly afterwards
Original company	Great Eastern Railway
Subsequent owners	LNER; BR
Currently managed by	National Express East Anglia
Station code	HPQ
Platforms in use	Three
Position	Through station on Manningtree to Harwich Town line
P&P	No 42, pp60-61
Services	Table 11: Liverpool Street/Manningtree to Harwich Town, with some services terminating here. Table 14: a few services from Cambridge/Bury St Edmunds and from Ipswich terminate here.

Above left: Looking towards Manningtree, a train arrives on 28 July 2009. Trains use Platform 2 for services to Harwich Town, as it operates as a single line. The station was built in 1972 and further enhanced in 1984. *Terry Gough*

Above : This shot of the station was taken from a ship leaving for the Baltic on 5 July 2009. *Terry Gough*

Left: An interesting evening photograph showing the illuminated entrance on 30 March 2011. *John Robinson*

HARWICH TOWN   37

Opened	15 August 1854; slightly inland and 300 yards south, new station opened 1 December 1865; 'Town' added 1 March 1883
Original company	Eastern Counties Railway/ Eastern Union Railway
Subsequent owners	Great Eastern Railway; LNER; BR
Currently managed by	National Express East Anglia
Station code	HWC
Platforms in use	One
Position	Terminus of branch line from Manningtree
P&P	No 12, p45; No 42, p63
Services	Table 11: services from Liverpool Street, Colchester and/or Manningtree.
Note	Branch known as 'The Mayflower Line'.

Above: The view along the platform from the buffers on 30 March 2011 shows the station building on the left and a Class 321 EMU ready for departure. *John Robinson*

Right: At one time there was an island platform to the left of this one, but after Parkeston Quay station was opened Harwich Town station lost a lot of its importance. On 25 October 1976 a Class 105 DMU awaits its 1100 departure time to Manningtree. Beside it is a car train with vehicles for export. *Author*

Above: The station entrance building on 30 March 2011. *John Robinson*

Right: The principal changes in this photograph of 14 April 2003 are the electrification of the line and the virtual closure of the freight sidings. The station building has not changed in the intervening 27 years, although the houses beyond the station are new. *Paul Shannon*

WALTON-ON-THE-NAZE   37

Opened	17 May 1867; sometimes known as Walton-on-Naze
Original company	Tendring Hundred Extension Railway
Subsequent owners	Great Eastern Railway; LNER; BR
Currently managed by	National Express East Anglia
Station code	WON
Platforms in use	One
Position	Terminus of branch from Thorpe-le-Soken
P&P	No 42, p57
Services	Table 11: services mainly from Colchester, a small number from Liverpool Street and some from Thorpe-le-Soken.

Above: On 30 March 2011 a modern unit, Class 321/3 No 321347, forms the 0900 service to Colchester. It is standing at the single platform, at the end of the approximately 5-mile-long Walton branch. *John Robinson*

Right: This is the station entrance and booking office on the same day. *John Robinson*

CLACTON-ON-SEA 37

Opened	4 July 1882; subsequently underwent various name changes
Original company	Clacton-on-Sea Railway
Subsequent owners	Great Eastern Railway; LNER; BR
Currently managed by	National Express East Anglia
Station code	CLT
Platforms in use	Four
Position	Terminus of branch from Thorpe-le-Soken
P&P	No 12, p44; No 42, p58
Services	Table 11: primarily semi-fast services from Liverpool Street, plus an occasional all-stations service from Colchester.

Right: On 19 June 2002 Class 321 EMU No 321310 awaits departure from Platform 2. There were four bay platforms in use at that time. *Author*

Below: This photo was taken on 30 March 2011, further back than the previous one, showing Class 321 No 321355 in Great Eastern livery at the same platform. The platform canopy can be clearly seen and there is no apparent change. *John Robinson*

Below right: An exterior view of the station, also on 30 March 2011, with a unit in the siding adjacent to Platform 4. *John Robinson*

SOUTHEND CENTRAL   37

Opened	1 March 1856; originally named Southend
Original company	London, Tilbury & Southend Railway
Subsequent owners	LMSR; BR
Currently managed by	c2c
Station code	SOC
Platforms in use	Four, of which two are bays
Position	Through station on the line from Fenchurch Street to Shoeburyness
P&P	No 42, p26
Services	Table 1: many services from Fenchurch Street terminate here.
Note	Station was refurbished in 2007.

Right: This platform view is looking towards Thorpe Bay on 9 November 2000. Platform 4 is a bay, as is Platform 1 on the down side. *Author*

Far right: Standing at Platform 4, unit No 310107 forms a departure to Fenchurch Street via Tilbury on the same date. *Author*

Below: The main entrance to the station, also on 9 November 2000. *Author*

Right: A later view of the line looking towards Thorpe Bay on 6 September 2006, with a very modern building on the left. *Roger Marks*

The refurbished entrance with ticket barriers, photographed on 6 September 2006. *Roger Marks*

SOUTHEND VICTORIA   37

Opened	1 October 1889
Original company	Great Eastern Railway
Subsequent owners	LNER; BR
Currently managed by	National Express East Anglia
Station code	SOV
Platforms in use	Four
Position	Terminus of line from Shenfield
P&P	No 42, pp41-42
Services	Table 5: frequent services from Liverpool Street.

Top right: The outside of the station on 16 April 2003. *Paul Shannon*

Right: This modern view from 13 July 2010 shows the side of the station in relation to the nearby shopping complex. *Author*

In this overall view of the station on the same day, looking towards the buffers, all four platforms are occupied by Class 321s. *Author*

SHOEBURYNESS   37

Opened	1 February 1884
Original company	London, Tilbury & Southend Railway
Subsequent owners	LMSR; BR
Currently managed by	c2c
Station code	SRY
Platforms in use	Three
Position	Terminus of line from Fenchurch Street
P&P	No 42, pp27-28
Services	Table 1: all services from Fenchurch Street.

Left: At one time the area to the left of the station was where Shoeburyness engine shed was situated, although apart from electrification the station itself has not changed very much, the three platforms remaining. On 16 April 2003 'Electrostar' Class 357/2 EMU No 357209 forms the 1652 service to Fenchurch Street. The single line to Pig's Bay (out of sight to the right of the car park) also remains. *Paul Shannon*

Below: The terminus building photographed on 6 September 2006. *Roger Marks*

Kent

Opened	1 June 1883
Closed	8 November 1914
Reopened	2 January 1922
Original company	London, Chatham & Dover Railway
Subsequent owners	SR; BR
Currently managed by	Southeastern
Station code	Two
Position	Terminus of branch from main line between Newington and Sittingbourne
P&P	No 20, p77; No 46, p110
Services	Table 212: frequent service from Sittingbourne.

Above: Class 508 No 508205 departs for Sittingbourne on 1 April 2004. The station has two platforms. *Terry Gough*

Below: By 4 November 2010, while the station is the same the unit is Class 466 'Networker' No 466014. *Brian Morrison*

Inset below: The modern entrance to the station is seen on the same day. *Brian Morrison*

MARGATE   14

Opened	5 October 1863
Original company	Kent Coast Railway
Subsequent owners	London, Chatham & Dover Railway; SR; BR
Currently managed by	Southeastern
Station code	MAR
Platforms in use	Four
Position	On coast line between Faversham and Minster
P&P	No 20, pp92-93; No 46, p101
Services	Table 194: terminus for services from St Pancras International. Table 207: terminus for services from Cannon Street. Table 212: through trains from Victoria to Ramsgate.

Top: On 28 March 1999 Class 365 'Express Networker' No 36502 awaits departure with a service to London Victoria. *Brian Morrison*

Above: The classical look of the entrance and frontage on 21 September 2011. *Anthony W. Smith*

Left: This view shows three of the four platforms with the rear of a Class 395 'Javelin' in the station forming the 1453 service to St Pancras International on 21 September 2011. It will head away from the camera towards Broadstairs and beyond. *Anthony W. Smith*

RAMSGATE   14

Opened	2 July 1926
Original company	SR
Subsequent owner	BR
Currently managed by	Southeastern
Station code	RAM
Platforms in use	Four
Position	Through station on Faversham to Minster Kent Coast line, but with certain services terminating
P&P	No 20, p90; No 46, pp97-98
Services	Table 194: St Pancras to Margate (through). Table 207: from Charing Cross (terminating) and from Ashford International (terminating). Table 212: from Victoria/Faversham (terminating).
Note	Station building is considered perhaps the finest in the New Classical style in the South of England.

Top right: 'Schools' Class 4-4-0 No 30939 *Leatherhead* leaves Ramsgate station on 25 August 1969 with the 2.41pm service from Margate to Cannon Street via Redhill. *Brian Morrison*

Centre right top: In the same scene 28 years later, 'Express Networker' No 365513 forms a Connex SE service on 29 August 1997, leaving for Charing Cross. The station canopies look the same but the chimneys on the skyline have gone. The old four-road depot also remains, although the individual tracks have been clearly numbered. *Terry Gough*

Centre right bottom: The attractive and imposing frontage of the station, seen on 21 September 2011. *Anthony W. Smith*

Right: The concourse is enhanced by light coming through the large windows, together with ceiling embellishments including the fine coat of arms of the Southern Railway. *Anthony W. Smith*

DOVER PRIORY   14

Opened	22 July 1861
Original company	London, Chatham & Dover Railway
Subsequent owners	SR; BR
Currently managed by	Southeastern
Station code	DVP
Platforms in use	Three
Position	Through station between Minster/Faversham and Folkestone
P&P	No 20, p86; No 46, pp88-90
Services	Table 194: terminating services from St Pancras International. Table 207: terminating services from Charing Cross and through trains from Charing Cross to Ramsgate. Table 212: terminating services from Victoria.

On 30 July 2002 Class 423 EMU No 3573 (Connex) is ready for departure using up-line Platform 2. *Author*

The attractive lighting enhances the modern entrance, photographed in the early evening of 6 September 2010. *Roger Marks*

South Coast

Opened	13 February 1851
Original companies	South Eastern Railway/ London, Brighton & South Coast Railway
Subsequent owners	SR; BR
Currently managed by	Southeastern
Station code	HGS
Platforms in use	Four (including one down-side bay)
Position	Between St Leonards and Ore
P&P	No 20, p75; No 45, pp107-108, 114-115
Services	Table 189: terminating services from Victoria, Brighton and Eastbourne. Table 206: terminating services from Charing Cross and Cannon Street.
Note	Many services terminate for operational reasons at the next station, Ore.

Above: Class 375 No 375905 awaits departure on 12 September 2007. *Brian Morrison*

Below: The modern-looking exterior of the station, photographed on 12 September 2007. *Brian Morrison*

Above: On 26 April 2001 Class 421/4 No 1837 departs as the 1444 service to Brighton. Two others of the same class are in the station, and semaphore signals remain at the far end. *Brian Morrison*

EASTBOURNE   12

Opened	15 May 1849; rebuilt 1866, resited 1872, and rebuilt again 1886
Original company	LB&SCR
Subsequent owners	SR; BR
Currently managed by	Southern
Station code	EBN
Platforms in use	Three
Position	Terminus, with Pevensey Bay to the east and Polegate to the west
P&P	No 20, p123; No 45, pp6, 82
Services	Table 189: terminating services from a number of stations including Victoria, London Bridge, Haywards Heath and Brighton.

Left: Two EMUs, Nos 1110 (left) and 1201, stand at Platforms 3 and 2 respectively awaiting their next turns of duty on 1 August 1987. *Terry Gough*

Below: The skyline visible in the first photo reveals itself as the front of the station, seen on 8 January 2008. *Roger Marks*

SEAFORD   12

Opened	1 June 1864
Original company	LB&SCR
Subsequent owners	SR; BR
Currently managed by	Southern
Station code	SEF
Platforms in use	One
Position	Terminus of branch from near Lewes via Newhaven
P&P	No 20, p6; No 45, p62
Services	Table 189: primarily services from Brighton with occasional services from Haywards Heath and London Victoria.
Note	Originally designed as a through station for an extension to Eastbourne that was never built.

Class 411/4 EMU No 1404 awaits departure to Brighton on 30 August 2000. *Author*

The exterior of the station buildings, also photographed on 30 August 2000. *Author*

A close-up of the end of the line on 29 April 2009. *Roger Marks*

BRIGHTON   12

Opened	12 May 1840; known at one time as Brighton Central
Original company	London & Brighton Railway
Subsequent owners	LB&SCR; SR; BR
Currently managed by	Southern
Station code	BTN
Platforms in use	Eight
Position	Terminus of three lines, from Lewes in the east, Three Bridges in the north and Ford in the west
P&P	No 20, p113; No 45, pp9-10, 12, 44-47, 50-51
Services	Table 52: from Bedford (FC). Table 123: from Filton/Bristol Temple Meads (GW) and Sundays from Cardiff Central (GW). Table 186: from London Victoria (SN). Table 188: from Littlehampton and various other departure points including Southampton Central (SN) and Portsmouth Harbour (GW). Table 189: from Lewes, Seaford, Hastings/Ore, Ashford International (SN).

Top: Class 159 No 159001 is seen leaving Platform 1 with a westbound service on 10 July 1996. In the distance can be seen a Class 73. To the right is part of Brighton depot (Lovers Walk). *Author*

Above centre: On 7 March 2003 Class 158 No 158864 departs from beneath one of the spectacular trainsheds. *Terry Gough*

Above: The station frontage on 13 October 2011. *Anthony W. Smith*

Right: An excellent platform view of Class 377/1 'Electrostar' No 377114 on 28 November 2008, forming the 10.49 Southern service to London Victoria. *Brian Morrison*

LITTLEHAMPTON   11

Opened	17 August 1863
Original company	LB&SCR
Subsequent owners	SR; BR
Currently managed by	Southern
Station code	LIT
Platforms in use	Four
Position	Terminus of branch from West Coastway
P&P	No 18, p94; No 45, p31
Services	Table 188: from London Victoria, London Bridge, Brighton, Bognor Regis, Portsmouth & Southsea, and Portsmouth Harbour.
Note	A new building, concourse and ticket office were constructed by NSE and finished late in 1987.

Left: Class 423 EMU No 3099, on the left at Platform 2, and Class 421 No 1715, on the right at Platform 4, await their next turns of duty. Looking from the buffers towards the main line (the branch is approximately 2 miles long), semaphore signals are still in use on 4 April 1992. *Terry Gough*

Below left: By 29 April 2009 the units are Class 377 'Electrostar' Nos 112 on the left and 412 on the right. *Roger Marks*

Below: An external view of the station taken on 7 July 2007. *Matt Davies, courtesy of Wikipedia*

BOGNOR REGIS   11

Opened	1 June 1864; original station destroyed by fire and replaced in 1902; 'Regis' added 1929.
Original company	LB&SCR
Subsequent owners	SR; BR
Currently managed by	Southern
Station code	BOG
Platforms in use	Four
Position	Terminus of branch from Barnham
P&P	No 45, p26
Services	Table 188: services from Barnham, London Victoria, and Littlehampton.

Top right: On 16 April 2002, looking towards the buffers, two Class 421s (No 1727 on the left and No 1846 on the right) await their next turns. *Author*

Below: The same view is largely unchanged in July 2009, with Class 377/3 'Electrostar' No 377325 at Platform 2. *Michael Mensing*

Right: The entrance to the station in October 2010, with the clock tower just in view on the extreme right. *Michael Mensing*

PORTSMOUTH & SOUTHSEA   10

Opened	14 June 1847; renamed Portsmouth 1876
Original companies	LSWR/LB&SCR
Subsequent owners	SR; BR
Currently managed by	South West Trains
Station code	PMS
Platforms in use	Four
Position	Part terminal and part through station
P&P	No 21, p16
Services	Table 123: services from Cardiff Central (GW) to Portsmouth Harbour. Table 156: both terminating and through services from Waterloo. Table 158: through services from Waterloo. Table 165: terminating and through services from Southampton and Eastleigh. Table 188: terminating and through services from Brighton, Littlehampton and Victoria.

Top: Class 20 No 20903 *Hunslet-Barclay* – with No 20902 at the other end – heads a special weed-killing train on 23 April 1997, standing on the lower-level Platforms 3 and 4. *Terry Gough*

Above: High-level Platforms 1 and 2 have an unusual trainshed roof, as seen on 13 July 1999. Class 421/5 'Greyhound' EMU No 1305 is on the left. *Author*

Below: The imposing front of the station, photographed on 6 March 2007. *Roger Marks*

PORTSMOUTH HARBOUR   10

Opened	2 October 1876
Original companies	LSWR/LB&SCR
Subsequent owners	SR; BR
Currently managed by	South West Trains
Station code	PMH
Platforms in use	Four (formerly five)
Position	Terminus of branch from Havant to the east and Fareham to the west
P&P	No 21, p17
Services	Table 123: services from Cardiff Central (GW). Table 156: from Waterloo (SW). Table 165: from Southampton/Eastleigh (GW/SW)
Note	Ferries are available to France, Spain, the Channel Islands and the Isle of Wight. A new passenger terminal opened in 2011, known as Portsmouth International Port.

Above: Looking along Platform 5 towards the buffers on 28 April 1993, the sign on the right gives directions for the Gosport Ferry and for the Isle of Wight. *Terry Gough*

Above: Part of the exterior of the station taken from one of the ferries on 6 March 2007. *Roger Marks*

Right: A view from the sea on 31 August 2011, with an Isle of Wight ferry by the dock. *Anthony W. Smith*

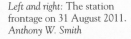

Left and right: The station frontage on 31 August 2011. *Anthony W. Smith*

LYMINGTON PIER 6

Opened	1 May 1884
Original company	LSWR
Subsequent owners	SR; BR
Currently managed by	South West Trains
Station code	LYP
Platforms in use	One
Position	Terminus of branch from Brockenhurst
Services	Table 158: shuttle service from Brockenhurst.
Note	Ferries depart for Yarmouth, Isle of Wight.

Above: This photograph was taken around 1950 from a departing ferry and shows the station and surrounds at that time. The signal box can be seen beyond and to the right of the platform. *Author*

Below: Jumping forward 37 years to 22 October 1987, we see the single wooden platform and Sealink ferry *Cenred* tied up on the other side. Only basic waiting shelters remain. *Author*

Above: On 23 October 2011 Class 450 'Desiro' No 450114 leaves with the 1044 service to Brockenhurst while Wightlink ferry *Wight Sun* prepares to depart for Yarmouth (IOW). *John Robinson*

Right: Having just arrived from Brockenhurst, Class 450 'Desiro' No 450114 forms the 1114 departure back there on 23 October 2011. *John Robinson*

RYDE PIER HEAD   6

Opened	12 July 1880
Original companies	LSWR/LB&SCR, although trains were operated by Isle of Wight Railway/Isle of Wight Central Railway
Subsequent owners	SR; BR
Currently managed by	South West Trains (Island Line Trains)
Station code	RYP
Platforms in use	One; originally four but number reduced when station rebuilt for electrification in 1967
Position	North-east coast of Isle of Wight, northern end of line to Shanklin
P&P	No 51, pp122-23
Services	Table 167: regular service to Shanklin seven days a week.
Note	Ex-LPTB stock is used; see also Shanklin opposite. Station is adjacent to terminal for Wightlink ferry service to Portsmouth Harbour.

Above and below: No 009 arrives at Ryde from Shanklin on 25 October 2001. *Author*

Above: The exterior of the station, photographed on 28 October 2011. *Howard Sprenger*

Left: This excellent overall view of the station is looking towards the buffers on 28 October 2011. One of the ex-LPTB units can be seen at the platform. *Howard Sprenger*

SHANKLIN   6

Opened	23 August 1864
Original company	Isle of Wight Railway
Subsequent owners	SR; BR
Currently managed by	South West Trains (Island Line Trains)
Station code	SHN
Platforms in use	One
Position	Southern terminus of line from Ryde
P&P	No 51, pp74-5
Services	Table 167: regular seven-days-a-week service from Ryde.
Note	Electrification took place in 1967.

Above: On 18 February 1998 one of the ex-London Underground tube trains, Class 483 No 008, arrives from Ryde. Six units have survived on the Island Line service since 1989; they used to run in NSE and 'dinosaur' livery, but from mid-2008 were returned to a replica of the original LT train red, with yellow fronts to conform with current safety regulations. *Michael Mensing*

Left: A view along the platform to the buffers on 28 October 2011. *Howard Sprenger*

Below: The outside of the station buildings on the same day. *Howard Sprenger*

SOUTHAMPTON CENTRAL   10

Opened	1 November 1895 as Southampton West, renamed Southampton Central in 1935, then Southampton in 1967 before returning to present name in 1994
Original company	LSWR
Subsequent owners	SR; BR
Currently managed by	South West Trains
Station code	SOU
Platforms in use	Four
Position	South Coast line between Fareham and Brockenhurst
P&P	No 21, p59
Services	Table 51: terminating services from Newcastle, Leeds and Birmingham New Street (XC), terminating services from Swindon and Westbury (GW), through services from Cardiff to Portsmouth Harbour and from Bristol to Brighton (GW), through services from Waterloo mainly going forward to Bournemouth/Weymouth (SW), and terminating services from Victoria, from Gatwick and from Brighton (SN).
Note	Following closure of Southampton Terminus near Docks in 1966, Central was rebuilt in 1967. There are plans to refurbish ticket hall, gate barriers and overall facilities.

The down side of the station has an almost art deco look of the far end. As can be seen there is a lot of renovation in progress on 15 January 2012. The bus is a free service to the city. *Howard Sprenger*

This overall view of the station looking west was taken on 15 January 2012. The 1015 service to Birmingham New Street awaits departure. *Howard Sprenger*

BOURNEMOUTH   5

Opened	20 July 1885 (2nd station); 'Central' dropped 1967
Original company	LSWR
Subsequent owners	SR; BR
Currently managed by	South West Trains
Station code	BMH
Platforms in use	Four
Position	Through and terminal station
P&P	No 29, pp30-33; No 44, pp92-96
Services	Table 51: primarily terminating services from Manchester Piccadilly (XC). Table 158: services from Waterloo to Poole/ Weymouth.
Note	Platforms 3 and 4 together form one of the longest in the country.

Above: Looking east from the station footbridge, Class 411/4 EMU No 1535 (leading) has just arrived from Waterloo on 24 July 2001. *Author*

Above: An overall view of the station on 20 November 2011, also looking east. *Howard Sprenger*

Above: Looking west, both through platforms are occupied on 8 September 1988. There is a short bay just off the picture to the right. *Author*

Right: The impressive down side of the station on 20 March 2011, with only yellow cabs in sight. *Howard Sprenger*

POOLE   5

Opened	2 December 1872 (2nd station)
Original company	LSWR
Subsequent owners	SR; BR
Currently managed by	South West Trains
Station code	POO
Platforms in use	Two (of which Platform 1 is bi-directional)
Position	Between Parkstone and Hamworthy on line to Weymouth
P&P	No 29, pp43-5; No 44, pp81-2
Services	Table 158: number of terminating services from Waterloo, and through services continuing to Weymouth.

Left: The modern-looking entrance to the station, photographed on 19 October 2011. *Terry Gough*

Below: Looking west towards Hamworthy on the same day, the entrance is on the up side of the line by Platform 1. *Terry Gough*

SWANAGE   5

Opened	20 May 1885
Closed	3 January 1972
Reopened	29 March 1987
Original company	Swanage Railway
Subsequent owners	LSWR; SR; BR; Swanage Railway (heritage line)
Platforms in use	Two
Position	Terminus of the heritage line known as 'The Purbeck Line'
P&P	No 29, p68; No 44, pp75-7
Services	During open periods trains run west/north-west to Norden.
Note	It is hoped that in the future services will be restored through to Wareham.

Above: The main entrance to the station. *Mark Hillmer*

Above right: On 24 July 2001, looking along the length of Platform 2, Class 33 No D6515 *Stan Symes* is stabled with a Pullman car. *Author*

Right: This wider view from January 2011 shows Platform 2 and the station buildings. *Mark Hillmer*

WEYMOUTH   5

Opened	20 January 1857, rebuilt 1986; at one time known as Weymouth Town
Original company	Wiltshire, Somerset & Weymouth Railway
Subsequent owners	GWR & LSWR; GWR & SR; BR
Currently managed by	South West Trains
Station code	WEY
Platforms in use	Three
Position	Terminus of lines from Dorchester South and Dorchester West
P&P	No 29, pp120-23; No 44, pp9-14
Services	Table 123: services from Filton/Bristol/Westbury (GW). Table 158: from London Waterloo/Southampton Central.
Note	Weymouth Quay station is out of use and NR has plans to permanently close the branch.

Above: Class 442 'Wessex Express' No 2413 (77418 nearest the camera) awaits departure forming the 1353 service to Waterloo on 7 October 1992. *Author*

Above: Class 31/6 No 31602 *Chimaera* stands at Platform 1 on 23 August 2003 with a regular Summer Saturday extra from Bristol Temple Meads, 'topped and tailed' with No 31468 at the other end. The service was still running in 2010 with Class 67s, and DMUs in 2011. *Terry Gough*

Above: The modern frontage of the station. *Terry Gough*

Left: Illustrating the length of the platforms, they are seen again on 1 February 2011. *Terry Gough*

South West

Opened	1 May 1861; resited close to original 2 May 1976
Original company	Exeter & Exmouth Railway
Subsequent owners	LSWR; SR; BR
Currently managed by	First Great Western
Station code	EXM
Platforms in use	One
Position	End of branch from St James' Park
P&P	No 8, pp42-3; No 52, pp66-9
Services	Table 135: terminating services from Paignton. Table 136: terminating services from Barnstaple/Exeter Central.
Note	The branch is known as 'The Avocet Line'.

Left: The exterior of the station on 18 September 2005. *Terry Gough*

Main picture: Class 142 'Pacer' No 142009 forms the 5.10pm service to Barnstaple on 10 October 2010. At one time the station was much larger, in contrast to the single platform of today. *John Robinson*

PAIGNTON   3

Opened	2 August 1859
Original company	Dartmouth & Torbay Railway, later amalgamated with South Devon Railway, then with GWR in 1876
Subsequent owners	GWR; BR
Currently managed by	First Great Western
Station code	PGN
Platforms in use	Two
Position	Terminus of line from Newton Abbot
Services	Table 51: primarily services from Manchester Piccadilly/Birmingham New Street (XC). Table 135: various services from Newton Abbot, Exeter St David's, Exeter Central, Exmouth, Cardiff Central, Birmingham New Street (XC) and London Paddington.
Note	Known as 'The Riviera Line' from Exeter.

Above: The station approach on 20 June 2000. *Author*

Above: 23 May 2007 was a beautiful Devon day, and from the road crossing at the northern end of the station we see Class 221 'Super Voyager' No 221131 in Virgin livery at Platform 2 with the 1403 service to Glasgow. The heritage line part of the station is on the extreme left beyond the white fence. *Author*

Seen from the other end of the station looking towards Exeter on 17 October 2009, Class 142 'Pacer' No 142063 awaits departure for Exmouth. *Terry Gough*

PAIGNTON QUEENS PARK   3

Opened	2 August 1859
Reopened	1973
Original company	Dartmouth & Torbay Railway
Subsequent owners	GWR; BR; Dart Valley Railway (30 December 1972), which became South Devon Railway
Currently owned by	Paignton & Dartmouth Steam Railway & Riverboat Co
Platforms in use	One
Position	Terminus at northern end of line to Kingswear
P&P	P&DSR Companion, p42
Services	Seasonal, with Santa Specials at Christmas.
Note	During the winter of 2011/12 the station building was demolished and a very impressive new one built, due to open at end of March.

Inset: The entrance to the heritage line station on 17 August 2004 – the platform is on the left-hand side beyond the white gate. *Roger Marks*

Main picture: The platform looking towards the buffers in October 2009. *Terry Gough*

KINGSWEAR   3

Opened	16 August 1864; renamed Dartmouth Ferry & Kingswear 3 April 1977
Original company	Dartmouth & Torbay Railway
Subsequent owners	South Devon Railway; WR; BR; Dart Valley Railway
Currently owned by	Paignton & Dartmouth Steam Railway & Riverboat Co
Platforms in use	Two
Position	Southern terminus of line from Paignton Queens Park
P&P	P&DSR Companion p81
Services	Seasonal, including Santa Specials at Christmas.
Note	Transferred from BR to Dart Valley Railway in 1972; DVR (Totnes to Buckfastleigh) subsequently split away and became South Devon Railway.

Above: Down at platform level, ex-GWR 0-6-0PT '6400' Class No 6435 has brought in a train from Paignton and is about to run round ready for the return trip on 23 May 2007. The Brunel Buffet Devonshire Cream Teas sound good! *Author*

Below: This superb shot looking down on the terminus was taken on 15 July 2007. The station board says 'Kingswear for Dartmouth' and the River Dart can be seen beyond the railway, with Dartmouth on the opposite bank. There are two platforms in use. *Terry Gough*

Above: The station entrance on 27 January 2011. *Richard Hillmer*

Below: The classic view looking west on 22 January 2002. From left to right can be seen Class 67 No 67023, a GW HST arriving from Paddington, a Virgin HST departing eastwards, No 47814 *Totnes Castle* with the 1150 service to Liverpool, Class 08 No 08499, and No 94337, a driving trailer

PLYMOUTH   2

Opened	28 March 1877; Plymouth North Road until 1958
Original company	GWR/LSWR Joint
Subsequent owners	GWR/SR; BR
Currently managed by	First Great Western
Station code	PLY
Platforms in use	Six
Position	Through and terminal station on Paddington-Penzance main line
P&P	No 8, pp124-5
Services	Table 51: services from Aberdeen, Dundee, Edinburgh, Glasgow, Newcastle, York, Leeds and Derby (all XC) and through services to Newquay or Penzance (some seasonal). Table 135: various services from London Paddington, Birmingham New Street (XC), Bristol Temple Meads, Bristol Parkway, Cardiff Central, Exeter St David's and Newton Abbot, with some through services to Penzance. Table 139: to St Budeaux Ferry Road and Gunnislake.
Note	Station was rebuilt starting in 1956 and officially opened by Dr Beeching on 26 March 1962.

converted for use in propelling mail trains out of termini. InterCity House dominates the skyline. *Author*

The scene at the west end of the station on 27 January 2011 includes XC Class 43 HST No 43027 on the left awaiting departure as the 1523 service to Leeds, and on the right an HST forming the 1506 service to Penzance (1206 from Paddington). *Richard Hillmer*

LOOE   2

Opened	11 September 1879
Original company	Liskeard & Caradon Railway
Subsequent owners	GWR; BR
Currently managed by	First Great Western
Station code	LOO
Platforms in use	One
Position	Terminus of branch line from Liskeard
P&P	No 17, pp25-6; No 54 p88
Services	Table 140: services from Liskeard (GW), no Sunday trains.
Note	Known as 'The Looe Valley Line'.

A plaque at the station commemorates Joseph Thomas. *Peter Townsend*

Left: The end of the line on 26 July 2011. *Peter Townsend*

Below: Class 150 No 150120 has just arrived from Liskeard on 27 July 2011 and will shortly make the return journey. *Roger Marks*

PAR   2

Opened	4 May 1859
Original company	Cornwall Railway
Subsequent owners	GWR; BR
Currently managed by	First Great Western
Station code	PAR
Platforms in use	Three
Position	On main line between Plymouth and Penzance; terminus of branch line from Newquay
P&P	No 54, pp73-8
Services	Tables 51 and 135: XC and GW services along Plymouth to Penzance line. Table 142: all services to Newquay. Seasonal additions.
Notes	Main station building is on down Platform 1. Line is promoted as 'The Atlantic Coast Line'.

Above: The main station building on the down side on 26 April 2001. *Author*

Left: Class 108 No P576 stands at Platform 3 awaiting departure for Newquay on 14 April 1977. The main-line platforms can be seen on the right. *Author*

Below: Looking west on 24 April 2001, on the left is a Penzance-bound DMU at Platform 1, and a Newquay service on the far right at Platform 3. *Author*

FALMOUTH DOCKS   1

Opened	24 August 1863 as Falmouth; 'Docks' added October 1988
Original company	Cornwall Railway (amalgamated with the GWR 1 July 1889)
Subsequent owners	GWR; BR
Currently managed by	First Great Western
Station code	FAL
Platforms in use	One
Position	Terminus of branch line from near Truro
P&P	No 17, pp120-1
Services	Table 143: all services on the branch.
Note	Closed from 1970 until reopening on 5 May 1975, giving passengers choice of three stations in Falmouth. Known as 'The Maritime Line'.

Above: A scene of change, photographed on 12 April 1956. *Terry Gough*

Right: The remaining single platform, seen on 12 August 2008. *Roger Marks*

ST ERTH   1

Opened	11 March 1852 as St Ives Road; renamed to existing title 1 June 1877 when St Ives branch opened
Original company	West Cornwall Railway
Subsequent owners	GWR; BR
Currently managed by	First Great Western
Station code	SER
Platforms in use	Three (one of which is a bay used for branch-line trains to St Ives)
Position	Through main line from Penzance to Plymouth and terminus of branch line from St Ives
P&P	No 17, p136; No 63, pp95-7, 119
Services	Tables 51 and 135: all services between Penzance and Plymouth (GW and XC). Table 144: all branch services to St Ives including a few that originate/terminate from/to Penzance.

Left: The St Ives bay platform is seen on 27 April 1996; the main-line platforms are on the left. *Author*

Below left: This view is taken from the down platform looking across to the bay (Platform 3), with a DMU awaiting departure to St Ives on 22 August 2005. *Roger Marks*

Below: The solid-looking station building on the same date. *Roger Marks*

PENZANCE   1

Opened	11 March 1852
Original company	West Cornwall Railway
Subsequent owners	GWR; BR
Currently managed by	First Great Western
Station code	PNZ
Platforms in use	Four
Position	Terminus of main line from Plymouth
P&P	No 17, pp140-3; No 63, pp104-8
Services	Tables 51 and 135: all services from Plymouth and beyond operated by XC and GW (which includes sleeper from Paddington). Table 144: a few services to St Ives.
Note	Platforms 1, 2 and 3 are covered by trainshed.

Right: A 'full house' on 5 July 1980, with Class 50 No 50013 *Agincourt* on the 0900 service to Paddington on the far side; another Class 50 is stabled further to the left. Semaphore signals were still in use at the time. *Author*

Right: Class 50s remain at work on 20 May 1984, with a Class 08 acting as station pilot and a Class 47 at the stabling point. *Author*

Top and above: Exterior views of the station taken on 19 August 2004. A stone by the down-side buildings is engraved 'Penzance welcomes you' and below 'Pensans A'Gas Dynergh', proving that the Cornish language survives. *Roger Marks*

Right: A Great Western HST awaits departure with the 1000 service to Paddington on 26 January 2012, while a CrossCountry Voyager is at Platform 4 forming the 0940 service to Manchester Piccadilly. *Richard Hillmer*

ST IVES   1

Opened	1 June 1877; resited 6 chains east at end of viaduct 23 May 1971
Original company	GWR
Subsequent owner	BR
Currently managed by	First Great Western
Station code	SIV
Platforms in use	One
Position	Terminus of branch line from St Erth
P&P	No 17, p139; No 63, pp126-7
Services	Table 144: full service on branch, with a few starting/terminating at Penzance.
Note	Last broad gauge passenger station to be built in UK; converted to standard gauge May 1892.

Left: On 5 July 1980 single-car Class 121 No 55026 (P126) is at the rear of the shuttle service that has just arrived from St Erth. The unit was built by the Pressed Steel Company and the 1978 Ian Allan 'Combined Volume' says, 'Single car or works with Class 149'. *Author*

Below left: An overall view of the station and its car park on 11 May 2008. *Terry Gough*

Below: Looking towards the buffers on 5 August 2010. Quite a few passengers await the next service. *Roger Marks*

NEWQUAY   1

Opened	20 June 1876; at one time called 'New Quay'
Original company	Cornwall Minerals Railway/GWR
Subsequent owners	GWR; BR
Currently managed by	First Great Western
Station code	NQY
Platforms in use	One
Position	Terminus of branch line from Par
P&P	No 17, p94
Services	Tables 51 and 135: seasonal services by XC and GW. Table 142: all services from Par.
Notes	Branch is known as 'The Atlantic Coast Line'. Station has experienced periods of growth and decline, having had two platforms at one time, both of which had to be lengthened to accommodate longer trains during holiday periods.

Right: The end of the single platform is seen on 12 April 2000, having been reduced from the original two. *Author*

Below: The outside of the station on 29 August 2009. *Geof Sheppard, with acknowledgement to Wikimedia Commons*

BARNSTAPLE   6

Opened	1 August 1854; formerly Barnstaple Junction, later Barnstaple for Ilfracombe and Bideford, before reverting to existing title in 1974
Original company	North Devon Railway
Subsequent owners	LSWR; SR; BR
Currently managed by	First Great Western
Station code	BNP
Platforms in use	One
Position	Terminus of branch line from Exeter
P&P	*The Tarka and Dartmoor Lines* (Terry Gough, 2010); No 8, pp72-4; No 53, pp4-5, 58-61, 71
Services	Table 136: all services from Exmouth and/or Exeter St David's.
Notes	Promoted as 'The Tarka Line'. Station has been much improved in recent times and now boasts excellent café and bookshop.

Above: Class 150 No 150233 waits at the single platform for departure to Exeter on 9 July 2003. *Author*

Above right: The station building, seen on the same day, shows a rather more substantial use in years gone by. *Author*

Right: The exterior of the station, photographed on 28 October 2011. *Howard Sprenge*Is the gull on the platform waiting for Bacon Baps to open? This is the view looking from the buffers on 1 August 2007. *Roger Marks*

MINEHEAD   7

Opened	16 July 1874
Original company	Minehead Railway (Bristol & Exeter)
Subsequent owners	GWR; BR
Closed	4 January 1971
Reopened	28 March 1976
Currently owned by	West Somerset Railway heritage line
Platforms in use	Two
Position	Western terminus of branch from Bishops Lydeard, near Taunton
P&P	No 30, p147; WSR Companion, pp72-93
Services	Regular services throughout the year between the two terminal stations, peaking in the summer months.
Note	Branch is 20 miles in length.

Above: Both platforms are occupied on 10 July 2002, with a green Class 115 DMU on the left and part of a loco-hauled train consisting of ex-GWR coaches in GWR livery on the right. *Author*

Above right: The end of the line – Platform 1 is seen on the same day. The unusual red items on the right are locomotive hoists; placed in position with a cross beam, they can lift engines so that wheel sets, etc, can be removed. They were originally used on Polish Railways and were brought to Britain by the East Lancashire Railway before the West Somerset purchased them. *Author*

Right: The entrance to the station on 9 June 2009. On the left can be seen ex-GWR 2-6-2T No 5553, and on the right an unidentified ex-BR 'Warship'. *Terry Gough*

WESTON-SUPER-MARE   8

Opened	1 March 1884 (3rd station); originally Weston-super-Mare General; present title adopted 21 September 1953
Original company	GWR
Subsequent owner	BR
Currently managed by	First Great Western
Station code	WSM
Platforms in use	Two
Position	Through station on a loop line off the Bristol to Exeter main line
P&P	No 16, p143
Services	Table 51: services between Manchester Piccadilly and Paignton (XC). Table 125: terminating services from Paddington. Table 134: from Gloucester/Bristol to Taunton, and terminating services from Bristol to Weston. Table 135: from Bristol to Penzance, Cardiff Central to Exeter/Paignton, Paddington to Paignton.

On 18 August 1994 Class 150 No 150234 awaits departure to Bristol. The view is looking west. *Author*

SEVERN BEACH   32

Opened	5 June 1922 for excursions, regular services from 10 July 1922
Original company	GWR
Subsequent owner	BR
Currently managed by	First Great Western
Station code	SVB
Platforms in use	One
Position	Terminus of branch line from Stapleton Road
Services	Table 133: all services from Bristol Temple Meads.

Left: Class 121 Pressed Steel Suburban No 55026 awaits departure from one of the then two platforms in use, forming the 1540 service to Bristol Temple Meads on Saturday 11 May 1985. *Michael Mensing*

Below: More than 20 years later, looking towards the buffers on 25 May 2007, the station is reduced to one platform, but with a modern waiting shelter. *Roger Cornfoot*

South and West Wales

Above: On 2 September 1994 Class 150 No 150270 awaits departure for Caerphilly, which was a regular destination from Bute Road, whereas by 2011 a unit shuttled to and from Queen Street. *Author*

Above: The old Taff Vale Railway HQ building remains close by the station entrance. Photographed on 16 September 2010, it looks in excellent condition, and is a Grade II listed building for various historical reasons.

CARDIFF BAY (Bae Caerdydd)   27

Opened	9 October 1840; various names – Cardiff Dock/Docks, Bute Road – before present title adopted 26 September 1994
Original company	Taff Vale Railway
Subsequent owners	GWR; BR
Currently managed by	Arriva Trains Wales
Station code	CDB
Platforms in use	One
Position	Terminus of short branch from Cardiff Queen Street
P&P	No 28, pp46-7
Services	Table 130: regular shuttle service from Cardiff Queen Street.

During the 1980s it was a railway museum. *Author*

Below: On the same date Class 121 No 121032 acts as the shuttle to Cardiff Queen Street. *Author*

PENARTH   27

Opened	20 February 1878; known at one time as Penarth Town
Original company	Taff Vale Railway
Subsequent owners	GWR; BR
Currently managed by	Arriva Trains Wales
Station code	PEN
Platforms in use	One
Position	Terminus of branch line that leaves Barry line south of Grangetown
P&P	No 28, p63
Services	Table 130: most services commence at Rhymney, Bargoed or Ystrad Mynach, and on Sundays from Cardiff Central.

Above: On 21 September 1994 Class 150 No 150277 awaits departure for Rhymney. *Author*

Above: There have been a few changes in the buildings beyond the station, but things remain much as they were on 16 September 2010, with No 150255 forming the 1302 service, also to Rhymney. *Author*

Below: Looking towards Cardiff, Class 142 No 142074 is working a Bargoed service on 16 September 2010. The seat in the foreground bears the GWR monogram. *Author*

Above: The entrance into the modest station building on 16 September 2010. *Author*

BARRY ISLAND (Ynys y Barri) 27

Opened	3 August 1896
Original company	Barry Railway
Subsequent owners	GWR; BR
Currently managed by	Arriva Trains Wales
Station code	BYI
Platforms in use	One
Position	Terminus of short branch from Barry
P&P	No 28, pp112-3
Services	Table 130: services primarily from Aberdare and Merthyr Tydfil, and also from Treherbert, Rhymney and Cardiff Central on Sundays.
Notes	In 1899 line was extended to Barry Pier station but subsequently cut back. Part of station area is now used as heritage line, Cambrian Transport (Barry Rail Centre).

Above: The signal is 'off' for the departure of a DMU towards Barry on 21 September 1994. The signal box (subsequently closed) can be seen at the far end of the platform used by Network Rail trains. *Author*

Above: The main station building is seen on 16 September 2011; only the entrance at the far end is used by ATW. *Brian Mills*

Left: The updated basic facilities of a shelter and train information screen now occupy Platform 1, used by Network Rail. Class 150 No 150260 waits departure for Aberdare on 16 September 2011. As can be seen, the signal arms on the bracket signal have been removed. Consideration is being given to the possibility of Network Rail extending the platform used by Arriva Trains Wales towards the tunnel so that six-car DMUs can be accommodated. *Brian Mills*

SWANSEA (Abertawe)   31

Opened	19 June 1850; formerly Swansea High Street, but returned to current title in 1968
Original company	South Wales Railway, amalgamated with GWR in 1863
Subsequent owners	GWR; BR
Currently managed by	Arriva Trains Wales
Station code	SWA
Platforms in use	Four
Position	Terminal station at end of short branch off South Wales main line between Cardiff and Carmarthen
P&P	No 37, pp9-14
Services	Table 128: services terminating from London Paddington (GW) and ATW local services from Cardiff Central, Manchester Piccadilly-Carmarthen/ Milford Haven, Swansea-Pembroke Dock, Cardiff Central-Fishguard Harbour. Table 129: terminating services from Shrewsbury via Heart of Wales Line. Table 131: services from Holyhead, Crewe and Manchester Piccadilly to Cardiff/Swansea.
Notes	Through services have to reverse. Refurbishment is planned for 2011-14.

Above: Looking towards the buffers on 4 April 1996, Platforms 1-4 (from right to left) are seen during a quiet moment. *Author*

Above: The exterior of the station building is faced in ashlar stone, as seen on 16 September 2010. *Author*

Below: A longer view of the platforms shows a Paddington-bound HST having just arrived on 16 September 2010. There are a few skyline changes from the 1996 photo. *Author*

The bright and cheerful entrance to the platforms includes a short summary screen of departures to Paddington, Manchester Piccadilly, Carmarthen and Pembroke Dock. *Author*

PEMBROKE DOCK (Doc Penfro) 29

Opened	8 August 1864
Original company	Pembroke & Tenby Railway, absorbed by GWR in 1897
Subsequent owners	GWR; BR
Currently managed by	Arriva Trains Wales
Station code	PMD
Platforms in use	One
Position	Terminus of branch line from Whitland
P&P	No 38, pp40-43
Services	Table 128: services from Manchester Piccadilly, Newport, Swansea, Carmarthen and seasonal from London Paddington (GW).

Above: Only the platform on the left is used, photographed on 9 October 2011. *Howard Sprenger*

Above: The station building is Grade II listed. *Howard Sprenger*

Class 47 No 47338 is at the head of one VGA, two KWA and six KFA flat wagons forming military train 6Z36 to Didcot on 11 April 1999. A rail-mounted ramp is used to load the wagons, using access from a nearby road. *Adrian Kenny*

MILFORD HAVEN   29
(Aberdaugleddau)

Opened	7 September 1863 as Milford, then Old Milford before existing title adopted 30 August 1906
Original company	Milford Railway Company
Subsequent owners	GWR; BR
Currently managed by	Arriva Trains Wales
Station code	MHF
Platforms in use	One
Position	Terminus of branch line from Clarbeston Road
P&P	No 38, pp52-54
Services	Table 128: services from Carmarthen, Cardiff Central, Newport and Manchester Piccadilly.

Left: This view of the single platform looking towards the buffer stops on 27 June 1994 shows the basic station facilities. *Author*

Below: On 27 July 2010 Arriva Trains Wales Class 175/0 'Coradio' No 175007 has just arrived with a service from Manchester Piccadilly. These units are all currently based at Chester. *Mark Chatterton*

FISHGUARD HARBOUR 29
(Porthladd Abergwaun)

Opened	30 August 1906
Original company	GWR
Subsequent owner	BR
Currently owned by	Stena Line
Currently managed by	Arriva Trains Wales
Station code	FGH
Platforms in use	One
Position	Terminus of line from Clarbeston Road
P&P	No 38, pp65-67
Services	Table 128: services from Cardiff Central and Swansea, usually two trains per day.

Above: Stena Felicity at the quayside awaits departure time to Rosslare, while units Nos 150275 (at the rear) and 150280 are seen arriving with the 1110 service from Cardiff on 27 May 1993. *Author*

Right: Looking from the end of the line, we see the full length of the single platform, also on 27 May 1993. *Author*

Below: This wonderful view is looking down on Fishguard station on 18 September 2010, occupied by Pathfinder Tours' 'The Western Wales Explorer' special, topped and tailed by Class 66 No 66015 (this end) and 'Deltic' No 55022 *Royal Scots Grey*. *Adrian Kenny*

Mid and North Wales and Wirral

ABERYSTWYTH   38

Opened	23 June1864; greatly extended 1925
Original company	Aberystwyth & Welsh Coast Railway
Subsequent owners	Cambrian Railways; GWR; BR
Currently managed by	Arriva Trains Wales
Station code	AYW
Platforms in use	One
Position	Terminus of line from Shrewsbury
P&P	No 32, pp120-1
Services	Table 75: services starting from Birmingham International/New Street, Shrewsbury and Machynlleth.
Note	Station is also western terminus of Vale of Rheidol narrow-gauge railway from Devil's Bridge.

Above: The station building is dressed with ashlar stone and has an attractive tower, as seen on 23 September 2011. A large part of the original station building is now occupied by Wetherspoons. *Author*

Above: The fully stocked 'Papurau Newydd' (news stand) by the platform entrances on 27 May 1994. The whole foyer area has now been completely changed – at the time of the photograph there were five platforms in use, including the VoR. *Author*

Right: The view towards the buffers on 23 September 2011. Beyond is a café area, with the unusual glasswork, and the tower appearing to the right. *Author*

Far right: On 23 September 2011 Class 158 No 158831 arrives at the remaining Network Rail platform forming the 0809 service from Birmingham International. On the extreme left is the part of the station in use by the Vale of Rheidol Railway. *Author*

PWLLHELI   49

Opened	10 October 1867; resited July 1909
Original company	Aberystwyth & Welch (sic) Coast Railway
Subsequent owners	Cambrian Railways; GWR; BR
Currently managed by	Arriva Trains Wales
Station code	PWL
Platforms in use	One
Position	Terminus of branch line from Dovey Junction
P&P	No 6, p86; No 36, pp24-6
Services	Table 75: departures to Machynlleth, where there are connections to Shrewsbury and beyond. On Sundays there is one through service to Birmingham International.

Above: Class 158 No 158840 stands at the busy platform on 28 April 2011. To the left is a siding used for light servicing, and to the right is a supermarket. *Author*

Above: The side of the station building photographed on the beautiful 28 April 2011 – the entrance is at the far end on the right. *Author*

Above: A close-up of the station entrance on 28 April 2011. *Author*

Right: On the same day Class 158 No 158840 stands awaiting departure time for Machynlleth, where a number of ATW Class 158 units are based for maintenance. *Author*

HOLYHEAD (Caergybi)   49

Opened	17 June 1880 (3rd station)
Original company	LNWR
Subsequent owners	LMSR; BR
Currently managed by	Arriva Trains Wales
Station code	HHD
Platforms in use	Three
Position	Anglesey – terminus of line from Bangor
P&P	No 6, p93; No 36, pp9-13
Services	Table 81: covers all services, from Euston (VT), Cardiff Central, Birmingham New Street/International and Crewe/Chester.
Note	The station is built into the Ferry Port from where there are daily sailings to both Dublin and Dun Laoghaire.

Above: In this photograph taken on 16 June 1988, before the new terminal building was built, we see how close the ships came to the station. Sealink *St Columba* has docked after arrival from Dun Laoghaire. In the foreground Class 47 No 47571 has been released by Class 08 No 08921 taking out the empty coaches of a London train. *Author*

Above: To the right of Platform 3 on 18 May 1993 can be seen the Freightliner Terminal, which up to its closure in March 1991 had four daily trains with containers bound for Ireland. Following the loss of this traffic it was redeveloped as a new reception area for vehicles using the ferries to Ireland. *Author*

Below: In this view of Platform 2, Class 158 No 158822 departs on 25 September 2010. *Author*

Above: The new terminal building is clearly seen here on 25 September 2010 as Class 57/3 No 57302 *Virgil Tracy* drags in 'Pendolino' No 390005 (from Crewe) forming the 0850 service from Euston. *Author*

Left: The inscription on the commemorative clock tower outside the station entrance reads 'Holyhead Old Harbour extension works commenced January 1878 opened by His Royal Highness the Prince of Wales 17th June 1880'. *Author*

Above: On 16 June 1988 three of the platforms within the four trainsheds with occupied. On the right is Class 150 No 150150 forming the 1530 service to Crewe, in the middle is unit No T326, and far left is No T338, both Class 116s – the 'T' referred to sets allocated to Tyseley depot. *Author*

Above: The central carriageway is very much a feature of the station, as seen on 26 June 1992. At the end of the platform is Llandudno Station signal box and to the left of it is a gantry with several semaphore signals. *Author*

Below: By 25 September 2010 the skyline has changed considerably with the demolition of most of the station buildings. Class 175/1 'Coradio' No 175110 awaits departure with a Manchester Piccadilly service. *Author*

LLANDUDNO   50

Opened	1 October 1858; new station 1 July 1903
Original company	Chester & Holyhead Railway
Subsequent owners	LNWR; LMSR; BR
Currently managed by	Arriva Trains Wales
Station code	LLD
Platforms in use	Three
Position	Terminus of branch line from Llandudno Junction
P&P	No 36, p38
Services	Table 81: services from Llandudno Junction, Manchester Airport and/ or Manchester Piccadilly. Table 102: services to and from Blaenau Ffestiniog, some of which start at Llandudno Junction. No Sunday service in winter months.
Notes	Central Victorian carriageway between main platforms is very unusual. There are plans for improvements that will include a refurbished concourse and improved wheelchair access, and original Victorian station buildings will be restored.

Below: This view of the front of the station on 25 September 2010 shows the remaining building and, to the right, the central carriageway entrance. *Author*

WEST KIRBY   51

Opened	1 April 1878; slightly resited in 1896
Original company	Hoylake & Birkenhead Railway & Tramway
Subsequent owners	Wirral Railway; Mersey Railway; LMSR; BR
Currently managed by	Merseyrail
Station code	WKI
Platforms in use	Two
Position	End of line from Liverpool
P&P	No 39, pp120-1
Services	Table 106: frequent service from Moorfields (Liverpool) Monday-Saturday, reduced on Sunday.

Above: Class 508 No 508115 awaits the signal to leave for Liverpool – the points are set for the train to take the up line out of the station. When photographed on 10 August 1990 the signal box and manual semaphores were still in use. *Author*

Right: Part of the original station is now a tearoom (right), with a traditional toy shop to the left. It is a very busy town centre with constant road traffic. *Author*

Below: On 23 July 2010 No 508114 departs for Liverpool, while a second unit has just arrived at Platform 1. *Author*

BIDSTON 51

Opened	2 July 1866, formerly Bidston Dee Junction
Closed	4 July 1870
Reopened	1 August 1872
Closed	June 1890
Reopened	8 May 1896
Original company	Hoylake Railway
Subsequent owners	Wirral Railway; LMSR/LNER (Wrexham branch); BR
Currently managed by	Merseyrail
Station code	BID
Platforms in use	Two
Position	Between Birkenhead North and Leasowe on through line to West Kirby, but also serves as terminus for line from Wrexham Central ('Borderlands Line', ATW), hence inclusion in this book
P&P	No 39, pp113-5
Services	Table 101: hourly service Monday to Saturday between Bidston and Wrexham Central, reduced on Sunday.

Above: Class 508 No 508108 is en route for West Kirby on 22 August 1989, although it shows 'Liverpool' on the rear blind. The junction semaphore signal is pulled off for the straight ahead route. To the right can be seen the top of Bidston Dee Junction signal box. *Author*

Below: The more recent photograph from 23 July 2010 shows Class 150 No 150257 forming the 1132 service to Wrexham Central. The signal box has been demolished and the semaphores have gone, replaced by colour lights; the box closed on 18 September 1994, and the lines then closed for a resignalling blockade until 3 October, when they reopened and Merseyside IECC took control of the Wirral Lines. The platform carries a nameboard that states 'Change here for the Borderlands Line'. *Author*

NEW BRIGHTON   51

Opened	30 March 1888
Original company	Seacombe, Hoylake & Deeside Railway
Subsequent owners	Wirral Railway; LMSR; BR
Currently managed by	Merseyrail
Station code	NBN
Platforms in use	Two
Position	Terminus of route from Birkenhead Park
P&P	No 6, p48; No 39, pp109-12
Services	Table 106: regular services to Liverpool Moorfields seven days a week.
Note	Line electrified in 1938.

Above: All lines are in use on Sunday 1 November 1987. A service to Liverpool is about to leave from Platform 2, as shown by the cleared semaphore signal and the lights showing on the front of the unit. *Author*

Right: The exterior of the station on 23 July 2010, visually unchanged over a long period. *Author*

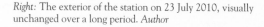

Left: Class 507 No 507009 has just arrived at Platform 1 on 23 July 2010. The semaphore signals have gone but otherwise very little has changed since 1987. *Author*

Above: One of the station nameboards promoting New Brighton's attractions, including an illustration of the fort by the sea. Known as Perch Rock Battery, building started in 1826 and was completed in 1829, mounting 18 guns. *Author*

North West

Opened	15 August 1836
Original company	Liverpool & Manchester Railway
Subsequent owners	Grand Junction Railway; LNWR; LMSR; BR
Currently managed by	Network Rail
Station code	LIV
Platforms in use	Nine plus Merseyrail underground
Position	Terminus of lines from Crewe and Manchester via Warrington Central
P&P	No 3, p57; No 39, pp6, 43
Services	Table 39: services to Stalybridge (NT) and Scarborough/Newcastle (TP). Table 49: to Nottingham/ Norwich (EM). Table 65: to Euston (VT). Table 90: to Wigan North Western (NT), Manchester Airport (NT), Blackpool North (NT). Table 91: to Birmingham New Street (LM).
Note	Station has underground Merseyrail platforms with trains to Ellesmere Port, West Kirby, New Brighton and Chester.

Above: The superb exterior of the station, photographed on 17 November 2011. *Author*

Above: On 1 November 2011, looking towards the buffers in the right-hand of the two trainsheds, an East Midlands Class 158 is at Platform 6 with a Norwich service, and local Northern Trains units are on the right. *Author*

Above: On the station forecourt are two bronze statues by sculptor Tom Murphy called 'Chance Meeting' between Ken Dodd, complete with 'tickling stick', and Bessie Braddock, the famous MP for Liverpool Exchange. *Author*

Left: The impressive span of the right-hand trainshed. *Author*

Right: A Virgin 'Pendolino' arrives with a service from Euston on 1 November 2011. Normally long-distance trains use Platforms 6 to 9. *Author*

SOUTHPORT   60

Opened	5 August 1851; known as Chapel Street until 5 May 1969
Original companies	West Lancashire and Liverpool, Southport & Preston Junction Railways; absorbed into LYR in 1897
Subsequent owners	LMSR; BR
Currently managed by	Merseyrail
Station code	SOP
Platforms in use	Six
Position	Terminus of Northern Line from Liverpool and line from Wigan Wallgate
P&P	No 3, p50; No 43, pp12-13, 17
Services	Table 82: services from Manchester Victoria/Piccadilly/Airport; on Sundays trains start from Stockport then via Piccadilly. Table 103: services primarily from Hunts Cross with a few from Sandhills and Liverpool Central.
Note	In 1970s former terminal building replaced by shopping centre, with station entrance, renovated in recent times.

Above: This overall view of the station shows Class 150 No 150135 leaving as the 1138 service to Manchester Airport on 10 June 2003. The Merseyrail electrics use the left-hand platforms, and DMUs the right-hand side. *Author*

Above: The modern entrance to the shopping centre as well as the station, photographed on 1 November 2011. The area in front of the station has been pedestrianised; it is close to the famous Lord Street shops and only a few minutes walk from the promenade. *Author*

Left: In July 2010 we see, from left to right, units Nos 507004, 508108, 156469 and 150140. *N. R. Knight*

Opened	30 May 1903; originally South Shore Waterloo Road, then Waterloo Road; current name adopted 17 March 1932
Original company	Preston & Wyre Railway
Subsequent owners	LYR; LMSR; BR
Currently managed by	Northern Rail
Station code	BPS
Platforms in use	One
Position	Originally on through line to Blackpool Central; platforms on coastal line added 4 July 1916 to replace South Shore. Ceased to be through station in 1964 when it became terminus of branch line from Kirkham & Wesham, following closure of Central station
P&P	No 3, pp22-3; No 43, p79
Services	Table 97: regular services from Colne, considerably reduced on Sundays with no winter service after early November; there are plans for a more frequent service.
Notes	Known as 'The South Fylde Line'. Station is only short walk from promenade and tram system.

Top: Class 142 No 142066 forms the 1244 service to Colne on 23 March 2011. On the extreme right can be seen where the lines to Blackpool Central once ran before the 'new' station was built. *Author*

Right: An overall view of the station looking south, away from the buffers. To the left is part of the huge car park that is fully used in the holiday season. *Author*

BLACKPOOL NORTH   60

Opened	29 April 1846 as Talbot Road; rebuilt 1898; replaced by existing station, on site of previous excursion platforms, 1974
Original company	Preston & Wyre Railway
Subsequent owners	LYR; LMSR; BR
Currently managed by	Northern Rail
Station code	BPN
Platforms in use	Eight
Position	Terminus of line from Kirkham & Wesham via Poulton-le-Fylde
P&P	No 3, p25; No 43, p86
Services	Table 41: services from Leeds and York (NT). Table 65: from Liverpool Lime Street (NT) and Manchester Airport (TP). Table 82: from Manchester Victoria (NT) and Manchester Airport (TP).
Notes	Became Blackpool's principal station after Central closed in 1964. Automatic barriers have been installed to reduce fare evasion.

Above: The well-known view of the station looking towards the buffers, with the Tower clearly seen. On 29 July 1993 there are three Class 150s at the platforms. *Author*

Above: A close-up of the terminal part of the station on 3 September 2010, with the new platform canopies. *Author*

Above: A view of the new barriers and part of the attractive station concourse. *Author*

Below: The front of the station on 3 September 2010, showing how compact it is. *Author*

Above: Five-car Class 180 'Adelante' No 180108 stands at Platform 8 on 3 September 2010. At that time three of these units were based at Newton Heath and used mainly on the services to and from Manchester Victoria to Blackpool North. *Author*

HEYSHAM PORT   60

Opened	11 July 1904 as Heysham Harbour; resited to east 4 May 1970
Closed	6 October 1975 apart from occasional use by boat train passengers
Reopened	11 May 1987 as Heysham Sea Terminal; renamed Heysham Port 1992
Closed	8 February 1994
Reopened	16 December 1994
Original company	Midland Railway
Subsequent owners	LMSR; BR
Currently managed by	Northern Rail
Station code	HHB
Platforms in use	One
Position	Terminus of branch line from Morecambe
P&P	No 43, pp102-3
Services	Table 98 (Winter 2011): only one train Monday-Saturday from Lancaster via Morecambe and no Sunday service (NT).
Note	Ferry service to Douglas, Isle of Man.

Above: On 19 August 2003 a Class 142 is seen arriving as the 1330 service from Lancaster. *Author*

Above: The view towards the end of the single platform on 17 October 2010. *Terry Gough*

Left: On the same date the ferry from Douglas, Isle of Man, is at the dockside. The ship is the SS *Ben my Chree* (*Girl of my Heart* in Manx) operated by the Isle of Man Steam Packet Company. *Terry Gough*

MORECAMBE   60

Opened	12 June 1848 (formerly Poulton-le-Sands); main station replaced by temporary station 4 November 1906 and permanent one 24 March 1907; Morecambe Promenade 2 July 1924; Morecambe 6 May 1968
Closed	8 February 1994
Reopened	6 June 1994 (new station)
Original company	Morecambe Harbour & Railway (Poulton-le-Sands)
Subsequent owners	Midland Railway; LMSR; BR
Currently managed by	Northern Rail
Station code	MCM
Platforms in use	Two
Position	Terminus of branch line from Lancaster
P&P	No 43, pp101, 104
Services	Table 36: regular services from Leeds. Table 98: all services from Lancaster including occasional trains that continue to Heysham Port.

Above: A Class 108 unit awaits departure from the old Promenade station with a service for Lancaster on 25 April 1984. *Author*

Above: Promenade station was virtually on the seafront, and is seen here on 19 April 2003 nine years after closure. *Author*

Above: The new station was built some 400 metres east of the first station. This is the booking office/waiting room building on 12 August 2010, unusually quite separate from the platforms. *Author*

Left: A view of both platforms of the new station, with Class 153 No 153316 awaiting departure as the 1232 service to Lancaster. *Author*

BARROW-IN-FURNESS   60

Opened	August 1846 as Rabbit Hill, replaced 1863 by brick building known as Strand, then Central; almost completely rebuilt following enemy action during WWII
Original company	Furness Railway
Subsequent owners	LMSR; BR
Currently managed by	First TransPennine Express
Station code	BIF
Platforms in use	Three
Position	Through station on Carnforth to Carlisle coast line
P&P	No 43, p121
Services	Table 82: terminating services from Preston, Lancaster and Manchester Airport (NT and TP). Table 100: northbound services, most of which go through to Carlisle (NT).

Above: Class 47 No 47441 departs with the 1310 service to Liverpool Lime Street on 14 July 1983. *Paul Shannon*

Above: The exterior of the down side of the station on 12 August 2010. *Author*

Left: Looking north towards Askam on 12 August 2010, Class 156 No 156429 stands at Platform 1 having just arrived from the south. Semaphore signals remain in use. *Author*

South West Scotland

STRANRAER

Opened	1 October 1862 as Stranraer Harbour; 'Harbour' dropped 1993
Original company	Portpatrick Railway
Subsequent owners	Portpatrick & Wigtownshire Railway (jointly owned by Caledonian, Midland, Glasgow & South Western and LNWR companies); LMSR; BR
Currently managed by	First ScotRail
Station code	STR
Platforms in use	One, although a second is available
Position	Terminus of line from Glasgow via Ayr
P&P	No 19, pp90-6
Services	Table 218 (2011): only six northbound services Monday to Saturday, three through to Glasgow Central, three terminating at Ayr or Kilmarnock, three on Sundays; six arrivals Monday-Saturday, three on Sundays.
Notes	Last ferry sailed to Belfast 19/20 November 2011, following decision by Stena Line to transfer operations to new deep-water port just north of Cairnryan. Thus no connection now between rail and ferries here. Proposal to move station a few hundred metres east, closer to town, to create rail/bus interchange, but no decision yet made. Stranraer-Ayr line known as 'The Galloway Line', promoted by Stranraer to Ayr Line Support Association (SAYLSA).

Above: At 7.52pm on 9 August 1973 the Larne ferry *Ailsa Princess* stands at the pier with the vehicle loading ramp raised in readiness for departure. On the right Bo-Bo diesel-electrics (later Class 27) Nos D5380 and D5366 stand with a Glasgow-bound service. On the far right is the signal box, which remains open in 2011. *Michael Mensing*

Above: Nine years later on 4 September 2002, looking towards the buffers, Class 156 No 156495 awaits departure for Glasgow Central. *Author*

Above: Looking from the buffers, at the right-hand platform are two DRS Class 37s, Nos 37601 and 37607, having arrived with 1Z94, a special from Glasgow on Saturday 12 February 2011. *Adrian Kenny*

AYR   77

Opened	12 January 1886 (3rd station, others 1839 and 1856)
Original company	Glasgow & South Western Railway
Subsequent owners	LMSR; BR
Currently managed by	First ScotRail
Station code	AYR
Platforms in use	Four (two through lines and two bays to the north)
Position	Through and terminus station on Stranraer to Glasgow line
P&P	No 19, pp100-7
Services	Table 218: services from Glasgow Central to Stranraer and from Kilmarnock to Girvan. Table 221: frequent services from Glasgow Central terminating at Ayr.
Note	Large hotel attached to station building.

Above: On 18 July 1984 Class 47 No 47098 departs with the six-coach 0745 Stranraer to Glasgow Central service, rather different from today's trains on this line, which are more likely to be two-car DMUs. The coaches are clearly marked 'Sealink' on the sides. *Paul Shannon*

Above: On 11 March 2005 Class 334 No 334008 stands in one of the bays with a northbound service to Glasgow Central. *Roger Marks*

Above: Part of the concourse roof with its beautifully designed wrought-iron supports. *Roger Marks*

Above: The outside of the station on 3 October 2011. *Richard Hillmer*

ARDROSSAN HARBOUR   77

Opened	Unclear; services from 1834; converted to standard gauge and connected to main network 17 August 1840; known as Ardrossan Pier, then Winton Pier GSW; then current name from 6 March 1967; resited 15 September 1986 when line electrified
Original company	Ardrossan Railway
Subsequent owners	Glasgow & South Western Railway; LMSR; BR
Currently managed by	First ScotRail
Station code	ADS
Platforms in use	One
Position	End of branch line from Kilwinning to Largs line at Saltcoats
Services	Table 221: regular services to Glasgow Central.
Note	Caledonian MacBrayne operates ferry service to Brodick on Isle of Arran.

Above: The entrance to the station is seen on 17 May 2007, with the ramp up to the platform then along by the buffer stop to the modern waiting room. *John Furneval*

Above: The ferry in the distance is the MV *Caledonian Isles*, one of the largest ships in the Caledonian MacBrayne fleet, able to carry up to 1,000 passengers and 110 cars. *John Furneval*

Below: Class 334 'Juniper' No 334016 stands at the platform with a Glasgow Central service in June 2008. *Anthony W. Smith*

LARGS   77

Opened	1 June 1885
Original company	Glasgow & South Western Railway
Subsequent owners	LMSR; BR
Currently managed by	First ScotRail
Station code	LAR
Platforms in use	Two
Position	Terminus of branch from Kilwinning
P&P	No 19, p112
Services	Table 221: regular services from Glasgow Central.

On 18 June 1993 Class 318 three-car EMU No 318257 leaves for Glasgow Central. *Keith Sanders*

Notes   On 11 July 1995 station and some nearby shops were largely destroyed when train crashed through buffers; rebuilding took place in 2005, although on a simpler basis. Caledonian MacBrayne operates a ferry service to Cumbrae Slip on nearby Isle of Great Cumbrae.

Above: Following the damage to the station in 1995, a modern booking office was built, as seen on 11 March 2005. *Roger Marks*

Above: Class 380 'Desiro' No 380116 awaits its return to Glasgow on 5 October 2011. *Richard Hillmer*

Left: The station entrance on 5 October 2011. *Richard Hillmer*

WEMYSS BAY   77

Opened	15 May 1865
Original company	Greenock & Wemyss Bay Railway, later incorporated into Caledonian Railway
Subsequent owners	LMSR; BR
Currently managed by	First ScotRail
Station code	WMS
Platforms in use	Two
Position	Terminus of branch line from Port Glasgow
P&P	No 19, p119
Services	Table 219: regular services from Glasgow Central (ScR).
Notes	1903 Caledonian Railway station building has unusual architectural qualities. Caledonian MacBrayne operates ferry service to Rothesay on Isle of Bute.

Above: The attractive station frontage, photographed on 5 October 2011. *Richard Hillmer*

Above: The platforms are seen here from the buffers on 7 October 2011, with Class 380 four-car 'Desiro' No 380101 awaiting return to Glasgow. *Richard Hillmer*

Left: The roof supports emanate from the unusual circular booking office, resulting in a fascinating effect. *Richard Hillmer*

GOUROCK 77

Opened	1 June 1889
Closed	5 February to 20 April 1973 for tunnel repairs
Closed	3 October 1993
Reopened	27 March 1995
Original company	Caledonian Railway
Subsequent owners	LMSR; BR
Currently managed by	First ScotRail
Station code	GRK
Platforms in use	Three
Position	Terminus of 'Inverclyde Line' from Bogston
Services	Table 219: regular services from Glasgow Central or Paisley Gilmour Street on Sundays.
Note	The station is considerably reduced in size since 1980s, but in more recent times has been renovated with completion planned for end of 2011.

Above: Class 334 'Juniper' No 334022 stands at Platform 3 on 30 September 2010. These units are painted in the Strathclyde livery of carmine and cream with a green waistband. *Mark Hillmer*

Above: The buffer stops at Platforms 1 (right) and 2 on the same day. A sign points to the Dunoon Car Ferry along Platform 1, a service operated by Caledonian MacBrayne; the crossing takes 23 minutes. *Mark Hillmer*

HELENSBURGH CENTRAL   77

Opened	31 May 1858; 'Central' added 8 June 1953
Original company	Glasgow, Dumbarton & Helensburgh Railway absorbed by North British Railway
Subsequent owners	LNER; BR
Currently managed by	First ScotRail
Station code	HLC
Platforms in use	Three
Position	Terminus of 'North Clyde Line' branch that leaves west coast line to Crianlarich just south of Craigendoran
P&P	No 31, p84
Services	Table 226: half-hourly service, mostly from Edinburgh, calling at Glasgow Queen Street (LL) (ScR on behalf of Strathclyde Partnership for Transport).

Above: This overall view of the station, taken on 14 September 1996, clearly shows the three platforms in use, two of which are occupied by Class 320 units. *Keith Sanders*

Above: The rather imposing entrance to the station, photographed on 10 March 2005. *Roger Marks*

Left: Two identical Class 318 units await their next turns of duty at Platforms 1 and 2 on the same day. *Roger Marks*

OBAN 83

Opened	1 July 1880
Original company	Callander & Oban Railway
Subsequent owners	Caledonian Railway; LMSR; BR
Currently managed by	First ScotRail
Station code	OBN
Platforms in use	Two
Position	Terminus of one of the branches of West Highland Line from Crianlarich
P&P	No 31, pp58-61
Services	Table 227: three or four services Monday-Saturday from Glasgow Queen Street, one or two on Sunday. In February 2011 it was announced that Edinburgh-Oban trains would run for ten Sundays, June-August 2011.
Notes	Small station building opened 3 January 1986. Caledonian MacBrayne operates ferry services to Mull, Lismore, Colonsay, Coll and Tiree.

Above: This well-known view, with the 'Folly' on the hillside beyond, was photographed on 27 March 2004. Class 156 No 156457 forms the 1235 service to Glasgow Queen Street, which is the return working of the 0812 from Queen Street. *Hugh Ballantyne*

Above: This photograph was taken from a ferry to Mull on 29 September 2007, with a Class 156 unit waiting departure for Queen Street. Usually trains combine with services from Mallaig at Crianlarich. *Author*

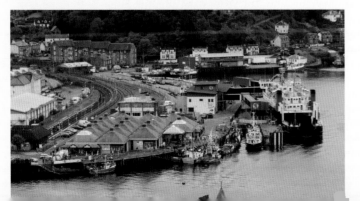

Left: The view from the 'Folly' looking down on the harbour on 23 September 2011 shows the station on the left and a ferry at the dockside on the right. *David Evans*

FORT WILLIAM   84

Opened	7 August 1894; resited half a mile north June 1975
Original company	West Highland Railway
Subsequent owners	North British Railway; LNER; BR
Currently managed by	First ScotRail
Station code	FTW
Platforms in use	Two
Position	Terminus of West Highland Line from Crianlarich; by reversal, trains can continue to Mallaig
P&P	No 31, pp110-2
Services	Table 227: normally four services a day Monday-Saturday including sleeper from Euston, others from Glasgow Queen Street, three of which continue to Mallaig. Reduced service on Sunday.

Above: Class 'K2/2' 2-6-0 No 61774 *Loch Garry* has arrived at the old station in about 1952, possibly with the 7.45am train from Mallaig to Glasgow Queen Street. *Author*

Above: After the new station had opened in 1975, Class 27 No 27003 waits with the stock for the 0940 service to Mallaig on 2 June 1976. *Author*

Below: The new station entrance on 20 May 2010. *Author*

Above: The new station is seen on 1 May 1995. On the right is a snowplough, and next to it the Motorail van off the sleeper., brought in by No 37430, which was then used for shunting. *Author*

MALLAIG   83

Opened	1 April 1901
Original company	West Highland Railway
Subsequent owners	North British Railway; LNER; BR
Currently managed by	First ScotRail
Station code	MLG
Platforms in use	Two
Position	Terminus of West Highland branch from Fort William
Services	Table 227: four or five services a day to and from Fort William and Glasgow Queen Street, Monday to Saturday, with a reduced Sunday service.
Note	Ferries depart to Isle of Skye and small isles.

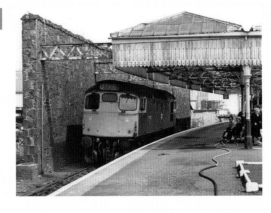

Above: Class 27 No 27003 has recently arrived from Glasgow Queen Street on 2 June 1976. *Author*

Above: A general view towards the buffers on 21 May 2010. *Author*

Above: The old station building is now mostly in use as a café, as seen on 22 September 2011. *David Evans*

Right: The view looking along the platform towards Fort William on 21 May 2010. *Author*

KYLE OF LOCHALSH   87

Opened	2 November 1897
Original company	Dingwall & Skye Railway
Subsequent owners	Highland Railway; LMSR; BR
Currently managed by	First ScotRail
Station code	KYL
Platforms in use	Two
Position	Terminus of branch line from Dingwall
Services	Table 239: four services a day from Inverness, one on Sundays.
Note	Since opening of the Skye Bridge, there are no ferry services from Kyle of Lochalsh.

Above: An overall view of the station on 25 July 1975, with Class 24 No 24124 shunting the yard. *Author*

Above: On the 18 August 1997 Class 156 No 156493 awaits departure as the 1520 service to Inverness. The layout has been considerably simplified. *Author*

Above: Looking from the buffers on 18 August 1997. *Author*

Above left: On 29 May 2006 a Class 158 stands at Platform 1 (west side) awaiting departure for Inverness. *Peter Townsend*

Left: At Platform 2 (east side) on 11 April 2007 Class 158/0 No 158712 forms the 1159 service to Inverness. Mist shrouds the Isle of Skye in the background. *Brian Morrison*

Northern Ireland

Above: The modern entrance to the station is seen on 13 September 2011. *Chris Playfair*

Below: On the same day, three-car Class 3000 No 3022 awaits departure. *Chris Playfair*

Opened	29 December 1852 as Waterside
Closed	24 March 1980, but building remains intact
Reopened	24 February 1980 (new station, considerably rationalised)
Original company	Londonderry & Coleraine Railway
Subsequent owners	Midland NCC; NIR
Currently managed by	NIR
Platforms in use	Two
Position	Terminus of line from Coleraine
Services	Regular service Monday-Saturday to Belfast Great Victoria Street, reduced on Sundays.

PORTRUSH

Opened	4 December 1855; replaced by extensively reconstructed station 1893; refurbished 2008
Original company	Ballymena, Ballymoney, Coleraine & Portrush Railway/Belfast & Northern Counties Railway
Subsequent owners	Midland NCC; NIR
Currently managed by	NIR
Platforms in use	One
Position	Terminus of branch line from Coleraine
P&P	*Irish Railways*, p114
Services	Regular service from Coleraine, some trains originating at Belfast Great Victoria Street; reduced service on Sunday.
Note	Relocation of station under consideration in 2011.

Left: On 13 September 2011 Class 450 No 8456 *Gosford Castle* approaches the station, passing the signal box at the south end of the platform and a somersault signal. Opposite are water towers and other semaphore signals. *Chris Playfair*

Below: This view of the terminal end of the station, with the old station clock in the background, was taken on 15 May 2010. *Chris Playfair*

LARNE HARBOUR   102

Opened	1 October 1862; current station 1985
Original company	Carrickfergus & Larne Railway/Belfast & Northern Counties
Subsequent owners	NCC; NIR
Currently managed by	NIR
Platforms in use	Two
Position	Terminus of branch line along east coast from Whiteabbey
P&P	*Irish Railways*, pp122-3
Services	Regular Monday-Saturday service from Belfast Central, reduced on Sunday.
Note	Ferries operate to Cairnryan and Troon (both Scotland) and Fleetwood (England)

Left: This platform scene on 13 September 2011 has Class 3000 three-car unit No 3021 at Platform 2 and a sister unit at Platform 1. The view is from the terminal end looking towards Belfast. *Chris Playfair*

Below: The station and port entrance on the same day, with Class 450 No 8452 *Olderfleet Castle* stabled on the left. *Chris Playfair*

BELFAST GREAT VICTORIA STREET   102/inset 101

Opened	30 September 1995
Original company	NIR
Currently managed by	NIR
Platforms in use	Two islands giving four faces
Position	Terminal station
Services	Suburban services to Bangor, Derry line, Larne and Newry, all terminating.
Notes	First Great Victoria Street station opened in 1839 and closed in 1976; current station built close to site of original. There are plans to improve infrastructure, including adding a fifth platform. It is expected that 'Enterprise' services will be transferred here from Belfast Central.

Above: Two Class 3000 units, No 3017 on the left and 3003 on the right, prepare for their next turns of duty. The photograph is looking towards the buffers. *Chris Playfair*

Above: A Class 3000 three-car unit departs on 29 August 2011; the buffer stops are immediately below the photographer. *Chris Playfair*

Left: The end of the line, with Platforms 1 and 2 to the right and 3 and 4 out of sight to the left. *Chris Playfair*

BELFAST CENTRAL   102/inset 101

Opened	26 April 1976; refurbished 2003
Original company	NIR
Currently managed by	NIR
Platforms in use	Two islands giving four faces
Position	Through station
Services	'Enterprise' trains to Dublin start and terminate here. Most other trains are through, although a few suburban services also terminate.

Above: This platform view taken on 13 September 2011 shows on the left Class 450 No 8457 *Bangor Castle* forming the 1142 departure for Larne Harbour, while on the right is 3000 Class No 3019 forming a morning service from Londonderry to Great Victoria Street. *Chris Playfair*

Right: The impressive exterior of the station in January 2012. *Chris Playfair*

BANGOR   102

Opened	May 1865; replaced by a combined railway and bus station 2001
Original company	Belfast, Holywood & Bangor Railway/Belfast & County Down Railway
Subsequent owners	NCC; NIR
Currently managed by	NIR
Platforms in use	Two
Position	Terminus of branch line from Belfast Central
Services	Regular services to Belfast Central.

Above: In this 13 September 2011 view looking towards the buffers, two Class 3000 three-car units await their next turns of duty. *Chris Playfair*

Right: The modern entrance to the station. *Chris Playfair*

Republic of Ireland

Opened	25 May 1844 about a quarter of a mile south-east of present station, opened 11 May; present title adopted 10 April 1966 to commemorate John MacBride
Original company	Dublin & Drogheda Railway
Subsequent owners	Great Northern Railway (Ireland); CIE
Currently managed by	Irish Rail
Station code	120
Platforms in use	Two
Position	Through station on east coast route
Services	'Enterprise' Dublin-Belfast trains and northern commuter services to/from Dublin Connolly, Dublin Pearse and Bray.
Note	Nearby is impressive viaduct over River Boyne, with stone arches and new steel girders replacing original ironwork during 1930s refurbishment.

The station entrance on 12 February 2009. *Neil Dinnen*

2800 Class 'Arrow' two-car units headed by No 2802 arrive at the station on 22 November 2008. *Neil Dinnen*

HOWTH (Binn Éadair)   95

Opened	30 May 1847 replacing Dublin & Drogheda station
Original company	Great Northern Railway (Ireland)
Subsequent owners	CIE
Currently managed by	Irish Rail
Station code	108
Platforms in use	Two
Position	Terminus of branch line from Howth Junction
Services	Terminating Trans-Dublin trains.
Notes	A DART station. There is no run-round facility.

DART 8100 Class No 8101 arrives as the 1340 Bray to Howth service on 31 July 2011. *Finbarr O'Neill*

DUBLIN HEUSTON   95, 96
(Stáisiún Heuston)

Opened	4 August 1846 as Kingsbridge; renamed after Sean Heuston 10 April 1966
Original company	Great Southern & Western Railway
Subsequent owner	CIE
Currently managed by	Irish Rail
Station code	1
Platforms in use	Nine (plus three LUAS); 1-8 are terminal, 10 is through (there is no Platform 9)
Position	Terminus of main lines from the south, south-west, west and north-west
Services	Intercity to Cork, and to Waterford, Galway, Limerick via Thurles, Westport/Ballina and Tralee; also south-western commuter services.
Note	Connected to Connolly station by LUAS light rail system and Phoenix Park Tunnel, which is usually used for freight and rolling stock movements.

Left: An overall view on 30 March 1992 includes Class 141 No 145 on the left and another of the same class on the right. *Author*

Right: On 19 August 2008 the trainsheds can be seen, and it appears that the platforms have been lengthened and have canopies. On the left stands 201 Class No 221 *River Fealge* at the head of an Intercity train, most likely to Cork, with Mk 4 green-liveried coaches. *Chris Playfair*

DUBLIN CONNOLLY   95, 96
(Stáisiún Ui Chonghaile)

Opened	29 November 1844 as Dublin; renamed Amiens Street 1954; renamed Connolly 10 April 1966 after James Connolly
Original company	Dublin & Drogheda Railway
Subsequent owners	Great Northern Railway (Ireland); CIE
Currently managed by	Irish Rail
Station code	100
Platforms in use	Seven (plus two LUAS), four of which are terminal from the north and three through
Position	Terminus of lines from east coast of Ireland and Sligo; connected to Heuston station by LUAS light rail system
Services	'Enterprise' service to Belfast, and services to Sligo and Rosslare Europort. Suburban services to Drogheda, Maynooth and Gorey/Enniscourthy.
Notes	In 1941 station took direct hit from German bomb; completely renovated and partially rebuilt in late 1990s.

Above: On 13 September 1994 NIR 111 Class No 112 is at the head of the 1100 'Enterprise' service to Belfast. *Author*

Above: On 17 August 2011 29000 Class No 29111 is on the left and 22000 Class No 22217 on the right with a service to Rosslare. Platforms 5, 6 and 7 are used for DART services. *Chris Playfair*

Below: On the same day an Intercity main-line service to Belfast is on the left (071 Class No 071) and to Sligo on the right (a 29000 Class four-car outer-suburban unit). *Chris Playfair*

BRAY DALY   95
(Bré Uí Dhálaigh)

Opened	10 July 1854 as Bray; two further name changes until present name adopted 10 April 1966, commemorating Edward Daly
Original company	Dublin & Wicklow Railway
Subsequent owners	Dublin & South Eastern Railway; CIE
Currently managed by	Irish Rail
Station code	140
Platforms in use	Three, two of which are in regular use
Position	Through station on east coast route to Rosslare
Services	Intercity Dublin to Rosslare, south-eastern commuter services and DART Trans-Dublin services; most southbound DARTs terminate here.
Notes	Series of paintings on Platform 2 depicts Irish history and Irish railway history from line's opening to 1960s. Station underwent considerable renovation under DART Upgrade project.

Left: 8600 Class DART unit No 8621 is stabled between duties on 17 August 2011. *Chris Playfair*

Left: An Irish Rail infrastructure vehicle is seen en route south towards Wexford on the same day. The signal box is at the far end on the right. *Chris Playfair*

GREYSTONES
(Na Clocha Liatha)   95

Opened	30 October 1855 as Greystones & Delgany; present name by 1922
Original company	Dublin & Wicklow/Dublin & South Eastern Railway
Subsequent owner	CIE
Currently managed by	Irish Rail
Station code	141
Platforms in use	Two, one of which has passing loop
Position	Southern terminus of DART electrified rail system, although some trains terminate at Bray
Services	Intercity Dublin to Rosslare, south-eastern commuter services and DART Trans-Dublin services.

Right: DART 8100 Class No 8121, at the head of a number of similar units coupled together, awaits departure on 25 July 2007. *Neil Dinnen*

Left: Another view of the station with DART 8100 Class units on 22 November 2008. *Neil Dinnen*

ROSSLARE EUROPORT   92
(Chalafort Ros Láir)

Opened	30 August 1906
Closed	14 April 2008 and replaced by new station
Original company	Great Southern & Western Railway
Subsequent owner	CIE
Currently managed by	Irish Rail
Station code	60
Platforms in use	One
Position	Terminus of line from Dublin
Services	From Dublin Connolly. Since 18 September 2010 single daily service from Waterford has been replaced by bus service.
Notes	There is a run-round facility at the new station. Ferries operate to Fishguard and to both Roscoff and Cherbourg, France.

Left: On 7 September 1992 Class 141 No 151 stands at the main platform of the now closed Europort station with the 1455 train to Dublin Connolly. *Author*

Right: There are tremendous changes between the old and new stations. Photographed on 10 July 2010, the latter is very basic with little more than a bus-style shelter. The unit on the right (No 2705) is on the now-discontinued service to Waterford. *Chris Playfair*

WATERFORD PLUNKETT (Port Láirge)   91

Opened	26 August 1864 as Waterford North
Closed	30 August 1906 and replaced by existing station; renamed Plunkett 10 April 1966 to commemorate Joseph Plunkett
Original company	Great Southern & Western Railway
Subsequent owner	CIE
Currently managed by	Irish Rail
Station code	50
Platforms in use	Four
Position	Terminus of services from Dublin and Limerick Junction
Services	Intercity services to Dublin and commuter trains to Limerick Junction.

Right: On 7 September 1992 Class 141 No 142 awaits departure with the 1515 Rosslare to Limerick train. *Author*

Left: IR 2700 Class 'Arrow' two-car diesel railcar No 2723 was photographed on 17 September 2010, the last day of operation of the service, which was replaced by a bus. *Chris Playfair*

COBH (An Cóbh)   90

Opened	10 March 1862 as Queenstown
Original company	Cork & Youghal Railway
Subsequent owners	Great Southern & Western/Great Southern Railway; CIE
Currently managed by	Irish Rail
Station code	66
Platforms in use	One
Position	Terminus of branch line from Cork
Services	Regular services from Cork.
Notes	Famous as station from where hundreds of survivors of RMS *Lusitania* disaster left town after sinking of ship.

Right: The station frontage was photographed on 29 June 1993. The building also houses the Cobh Heritage Centre, which records emigration and famine between 1848 and 1950. More than 6 million adults and children emigrated from Ireland, 2.5 million of whom departed from Cobh. *Author*

Right: On 11 January 2012 2600 Class 'Arrow' two-car units Nos 2614 and 2617 await time to return to Cork with the 1330 service. The Heritage Centre can be seen in the background. *Finbarr O'Neill*

CORK KENT (Corcaigh Stáisiún Kent)   90

Opened	2 February 1893 as Glanmire Road; present name adopted 10 April 1966, commemorating Thomas Kent
Original company	Cork & Youghal Railway, taken over by Great Southern & Western Railway 1865; current station replaced those of the two companies
Subsequent owner	Great Southern & Western Railway; CIE
Currently managed by	Irish Rail
Station code	30
Platforms in use	Five
Position	Primarily a terminal station between Glounthaune and Mallow
Services	Intercity services from Dublin and Tralee and commuter services to Mallow, Cobh and Midleton.

Left: 'A' Class No 055 is at the head of the 0820 train to Mallow on 26 September 1993. Only one of these locomotives remains, now in preservation. *Author*

Right: On the left is the Cork to Swansea ferry, then a Cork to Dublin Intercity train, while on the right is a Cobh and Midleton commuter service, photographed on 18 August 2011. *Chris Playfair*

TRALEE CASEMENT (Trá Lí)   89

Opened	18 July 1859 as Tralee South; renamed 10 April 1966 commemorating Roger Casement
Original company	Tralee & Killarney Railway
Subsequent owners	Great Southern & Western; CIE
Currently managed by	Irish Rail
Station code	28
Platforms in use	One
Position	Terminus of line from Mallow
Services	Intercity services from Dublin and Cork, commuter services from Mallow.

Above: 8 June 1993 071 Class No 074 heads the 1420 train to Dublin Heuston. *Author*

Above: The end of the line on 22 May 2010 – when most trains were locomotive-hauled they needed the headshunt to run round their train, but since the introduction of the new Korean-built Intercity railcars the headshunt is no longer required and has been removed. *Chris Playfair*

Above: The signal box is seen on 28 June 1993 and on 18 August 2011 as preserved – the tracks have gone but the gate beyond remains. The box became redundant in 2005. *Author/ Chris Playfair*

Above: Looking from the station towards Killarney on 22 May 2010, a locomotive-hauled charter special is about to depart for Belfast. The loco had to shunt to the yard in order to run round the coaches – ten years earlier it would have been a simple run in and around and ready to go! *Chris Playfair*

LIMERICK COLBERT (Luimneach)   93

Opened	28 August 1858 as Limerick; renamed 10 April 1966 commemorating Cornelius Colbert
Original company	Waterford & Limerick Railway
Subsequent owners	Great Southern & Western; CIE
Currently managed by	Irish Rail
Station code	40
Platforms in use	Four
Position	Terminus of line from Killonan Junction
Services	Intercity services to Dublin and Galway, commuter lines to Nenagh/Ballybrophy and to Ennis, and shuttle to Limerick Junction.
Note	Possibility that Irish Rail may seek permission to close Ballybrophy line.

Left: The imposing station frontage, photographed on 9 August 2005. *Matthew Crockett*

Below: 071 Class No 083 in the new black and silver 'freight' livery stands at the head of an Intercity service to Dublin on 24 April 2010. Four locos of this class retain their black and orange IE livery. *Chris Playfair*

GALWAY CEANNT (Stáisiún Cheannt)   93

Opened	1 August 1851; renamed 10 April 1966 commemorating Eamonn Ceannt
Original company	Midland Great Western Railway
Subsequent owner	CIE
Currently managed by	Irish Rail
Station code	170
Platforms in use	Two
Position	Terminus of branch line from Athlone East Junction
Services	Intercity services to Dublin and Limerick and Galway Suburban Rail commuter services.
Note	There are plans to redevelop station.

Top left: The Hotel Meyrick, formerly the Great Southern Hotel, provides an impressive frontage to the station in the heart of Galway City, also photographed on 1 May 2011. *Neil Dinnen*

Above: Nos 22003 and 22006 (left) have arrived with the 0830 service from Heuston on the same day. No 22131 is in the siding and will later form the 1505 Heuston service. *Neil Dinnen*

Above: A most unusual scene with a number of DMU sets in view. From left to right we have 22020, next are 2701+2702, behind them is 22027 which will be working the 1630 to Heuston Special on Monday, then 22031 on the 1505 to Heuston, next 22006+22003 are working the 1305 to Dublin and finally 2707+2708 forming the 1205 to Limerick. Taken on Sunday 1 May 2011. *Neil Dinnen*

WESTPORT (Cathair na Mart)   97

Opened	28 January 1866; formerly known as Westport Town c1875; present name adopted by 1904
Original company	Great Northern & Western Railway
Subsequent owners	Midland Great Western Railway; CIE
Currently managed by	Irish Rail
Station code	169
Platforms in use	Two
Position	Terminus of short branch from Manulla Junction
Services	Intercity services from Dublin Heuston.

078 Class No 078 is at the head of a train that arrived from Athlone at Sunday lunchtime on 13 July 2008 and is waiting to depart as the 1425 service to Dublin. At one time the railway continued to Westport Quay and Achill. *Chris Playfair*

BALLINA (Béal an Átha)   97

Opened	19 May 1873
Original company	Great Northern & Western Railway
Subsequent owners	Midland Great Western Railway; CIE
Currently managed by	Irish Rail
Station code	167
Platforms in use	One
Position	Terminus of branch line from Manulla Junction
Services	Intercity services from Dublin Heuston.
Note	Run-round facility available.

On 8 September 1992 181 Class No 181 has arrived from Manulla Junction. The windsock was in connection with a nearby chemical plant. *Author*

On 22 February 2006 a similar view at Ballina shows a three-coach service awaiting departure. It is believed that the windsock was removed a number of years earlier. *Matthew Crockett*

SLIGO MAC DIARMADA (Stáisiún Sheáin Mhic Dhiarmada)   98

Opened	3 December 1862; replaced by 2nd station July 1863; renamed 10 April 1966 commemorating Mac Diarmada
Original company	Midland Great Western Railway
Subsequent owner	CIE
Currently managed by	Irish Rail
Station code	180
Platforms in use	One, second available
Position	Most northerly terminus, end of line from Dublin
Services	Intercity services from Dublin Connolly.

071 Class No 078 arrives with a charter special on 7 March 2010. *Chris Playfair*

Index of Locations